NEEDING NORMAL

★ ★ ★ ★ ★

"Inspiring and empowering, this young adult novel explores the true sense of friendship and acceptance. It is a brilliant novel with outstanding protagonists and a powerful message that leaves you feeling that our world is evolving into a more understanding and wonderful place."

Susan Sewell for *Readers' Favorite*

★ ★ ★ ★ ★

"…the storyline is wonderful, and it is definitely an appropriate must-read for teens and adults."

Vincent Dublado for *Readers' Favorite*

★ ★ ★ ★ ★

"Needing Normal is an absorbing character-driven drama that will entertain teenagers and adults alike. Jett is a riveting protagonist that you instantly start rooting for… The plot is a slow burn, yet you can't take your eyes off the pages."

Pikasho Deka for *Readers' Favorite*

★ ★ ★ ★ ★

"Jett is a voice for a generation beset with expectations from every angle, and utilizing her struggle for normality at the core of the novel produces a very poignant message for young adult readers today... I would highly recommend Needing Normal: Freshman Year to fans of gentle coming-of-age works, poignant social issues writing, and teen drama fans everywhere."

K.C. Finn for *Readers' Favorite*

★ ★ ★ ★ ★

"Needing Normal by Emme Grange was such a powerful and relatable read for me. As someone who is on the spectrum, I could definitely identify with the struggles that Jett faced... I think a lot of people on that spectrum can relate to Jett. She is so well written that you find yourself stepping into her shoes... Emme Grange has written an amazing novel and I cannot wait to see what else she writes."

Tiffany Ferrell for *Readers' Favorite*

Emme Grange

NEEDING NORMAL
Freshman Year

Needing Normal
Freshman Year

Copyright © 2021
by aTYPICAL AUTHOR press for Emme Grange.

All rights reserved.

aTYPICAL AUTHOR press supports the integrity of intellectual property and the value of copyright. The purpose of copyright is to encourage individuals to produce the creative works that enrich our culture.

ANY distribution of an authors' intellectual property without their express written permission, other than limited excerpts for review purposes, is considered theft and expressly prohibited.

If you would like to obtain permission to use material from this book or any other works by Emme Grange, please contact talksoon@atypicalauthor.com for consideration. Thank you for your support of the author's rights.

Cover design by Cover Culture
Interior formatting by Alt 19 Creative

ISBN 978-1-955856-00-3 (hc) / 978-1-955856-01-0 (pb) / 978-1-955856-02-7 (e) / 978-1-955856-03-4 (a)

Published by:

aTYPICAL
AUTHOR
press

Daddio was real. Thirty-five years ago, he told me to tell the stories. He said you needed them, too. So here we are. Daddio, this one is for you.
(July 29, 1936–February 8, 2021)

NEEDING NORMAL

IF YOU WERE JETT HARPER, you would know you are normal, and it is very, very good. You would know this and be grateful, because nothing disproved your knowledge. You would celebrate your fourteenth birthday knowing it is the beginning of a new era, full of promising possibilities. If you were Jett, you would be happy the school year approached. Pretty soon you would continue being the best in your class, arguably the best in your school. That is what you would expect from freshman life at Presidio Prep. And that is how it would feel to be Jett Harper... until you learned otherwise.

———⟩•⟨———

ON THE END OF A QUAINT CUL-DE-SAC, in the quiet of Tiburon near Blackie's Pasture, Jett was in her room, getting ready for the first day of school. Her parents' whispered argument caught Jett's full attention. Wait. Either someone had misspoken or she'd missed a word. Of course she missed a word. What she'd heard just didn't make sense. It couldn't be right. Jett stilled to listen more carefully.

"Joe, I don't think she's ready," said Jett's mother. "We're setting her up to fail."

"How so?" demanded Jett's dad. "Tell me exactly."

Mother took a breath and continued. "I'm telling you she's not ready. In my office, I see kids like her every day—kids you might never expect to be struggling."

"Mmm-hmm, but she's not in your office. She's our daughter." Daddio was in interrogation mode. "How are we setting our brilliant girl up to fail by sending her to the best high school in the state?"

Mother wasn't backing down. "It's too much pressure. The kids I see? They're depressed. They're anxious. Some of them have disappeared and come back traumatized. Do you want that to be her? Do you want those parents to be us?"

Jett heard disbelief color Daddio's tone. "Oh, come on, Kathy! Really?" The rhythmic thump of footfalls punctuated his message as he paced. "You know I had to call in favors to even get her an interview, right? And in case you've forgotten, high school is where people start making connections that stay with them for the rest of their lives."

"Exactly my point. Pressure," Mother said.

"Well, I'm telling you, I may have gotten her a spot to be *considered,* but Jett actually *nailed* the admissions process. She's a natural!"

"Look, I know you think I'm paranoid, but I've spent years studying so I could give our child the emotional equivalent of your intellectual boost. And I'm telling you, I know in my gut. Something is wrong."

Jett frowned at this, but kept listening. Mother sounded so sure of her opinion as she continued.

"Need an example? Jett and I should have gone back-to-school shopping together, bonding over fashion and french fries. Instead, once again, she refused to shop with me. She snubbed mani/pedis, shopping, the works! What girl *does* that?"

Jett thought that was a no-brainer. Girls with things to do. Jett had spent her valuable time getting ready for high school. There had been so much to research. Plus, who wanted to shop in person? Why not just order your favorite things to wear in multiples and be done with it?

While Mother waited for Daddio to answer, the beat of silence lasted too long.

Jett moved closer to her door, knowing whatever came next would be significant. With practiced patience, she carefully and quietly cracked it open. She knew she wasn't supposed to listen in, but how could she not? She found her parents' rare disagreements fascinating.

Jett imagined she heard the change in Mother's breathing even before hearing her voice. Someone's deep sigh punctuated the pregnant silence. Were they still considering "what girl does that"?

In a rumble that resembled a growl, Mother insisted, "She's *not* normal!"

For half a moment while the entire world realigned, Jett froze. Then she backed up. Silence screamed. There was nothing more to hear.

Jett's brain spun. Not normal? What? Her mother was at it again, bringing home the residue of recent work from her counseling practice. But just in case, she jumped on her computer and quickly researched girls' development at age fourteen. She looked at common data and took a few cursory "tests," knowing there was little scientific significance. Social and emotional development could not be measured like hard facts. Psychology and sociology were not real sciences. Jett thought about the results. She fell well within range on all the physical development charts. That mattered. It was real, relevant data. Data made her feel better. She *was* normal. Phew!

And, in light of Mother's faulty revelation, Jett reconsidered what to wear for the first day of high school. She could not fathom wearing either of the outfits Mother had chosen for her, not on her first day at Presidio Prep, not on her last. She tried to get excited about the brightly colored dress, or at least tolerate the garish pants and top.

But how? Jett picked up the metallic belt. Maybe she could incorporate this into her outfit? Nope. She put it back down and waltzed into her parents' room so she could "borrow" one of Daddio's dress shirts.

"Lovebug, are you in there?" Jett's dad caught her red-handed, rummaging through his closet. "What are you doing, kiddo?"

"I need a shirt. I'm thinking one of your casual button-downs will work nicely."

Daddio's forehead wrinkled. "Didn't your mother get you the latest and greatest for your first day? And you know, I think there's a bit of a size difference between us..."

Jett grinned. "Yeah, Daddio. You know she did and there is. But honestly? Who's gonna take me seriously if I show up looking like I just stepped off some fashion runway? I want to fit in, not stand out!"

"Bug, you know what I'm going to say to that... Say it with me."

Jett, in a huff, and Daddio, with enthusiasm, quoted Dr. Seuss. *"Why fit in when you were born to stand out?"*

Smiling at his lack of understanding, Jett took a shirt off the hanger, kissed his cheek, and walked out. He was such an *extra* extrovert!

Jett returned to her room. She slipped into her cuffed Levi's and the oversized dress shirt. She rolled up the sleeves. After stepping into new canvas sneakers, she tried to decide between a sweater or a hoodie and went with the latter. Mother would have chosen the sweater.

Mother entered her room without knocking. "How'd it... Oh." Mother crossed her arms, and Jett turned around. Her mother tried again. "So, I see you found your own... style?" She squinted and started nodding slowly as if trying to understand.

Jett felt a little bad. "Yeah, sorry. I know you really thought through the whole soft-texture, no-tag thing. That means a lot to me, and yet I just..." She paused, trying to figure out how to soften the message. "I just couldn't... you know? I spent the entire summer studying so I would be ready for this rite of passage known as high school. I really want to show up brains over beauty and function over fashion. Mixing with peers who may finally be on my level? I am really excited! Can you just be happy for me?"

Jett looked up but couldn't meet Mother's eyes. Their relationship had been strained before. Being on different pages wasn't new in their dynamic, but now the air clouded with an acute ache of... something. What was it? Jett felt compelled to figure it out.

She looked down at her outfit. Everything seemed in order—everything except for the doubts planted by that intense, whispered confrontation. She couldn't stop her mind from another replay. Wandering back through the memory, Jett tried hard to understand as she felt the tic in her jaw begin.

"Um, okay, I'll meet you downstairs." Mother left her alone to finish getting ready.

Jett tried to recapture some of the excitement she'd felt before overhearing her parents. She got busy organizing her assignments and supplies into the Mad Pax she treasured. It was go time. Jett looked down at her bag. She saw the new Spiketus Rex that Uncle Darren had given her for her birthday and smiled.

At the little family party, Mother had pulled her aside to explain that being a workaholic man with no family, Darren simply didn't know what to get a teenage girl. Mother reminded her that even so, it was her duty to be kind to her adoptive uncle. Her mother further explained that Jett didn't have to carry it anywhere. Jett balked at her mother's reaction to her new backpack. All Jett could think was how lucky she was to have a bag that roared "leave my work alone!" Darren's choice was spot-on, and she couldn't wait to carry it as her statement piece.

Mother would hate that, too. For a second Jett considered exchanging it for some other carryall bag in her closet, one that Mother would choose, but then reason returned. Even if it wasn't the statement piece her mother would reach for, it still followed her tenets. Jett's treasured backpack, with its soft yet spiky scales, clearly said something about the carrier and had a function. That meant it satisfied all requirements. Jett was proud of herself for considering Mother's philosophies and honoring them.

"Dad! Mom! I'm ready! We need to go, right?" Jett hopped down the stairs and into the hallway.

Suddenly there was frenetic motion, like the world had started again. Jett listened to the hum of home winding into a new day.

"Um, yeah! You got it, Doodlebug! Time to go," Daddio responded.

Right behind Daddio, Mother came out of the kitchen with a too-bright smile and a too-hot breakfast. She offered both to Jett as she chirped, "Let's get going! Big day! Are you ready?"

Mother was trying hard to sound casual and enthusiastic. It only emphasized her earlier, ugly admission.

"Mom! I'll be fine!" Jett rolled her eyes, knowing it was a response a typical teen would give. She'd seen it enough times in movies, media, and real life.

Jett jumped into the back of Daddio's car. She liked Mother's better, but she also knew there was no point in arguing. They would be taking his stuffy old car today instead of the newer, sleeker one. It was Monday, and Daddio always drove on Mondays. Waiting to crack the window, Jett smiled to herself. The adventure was about to begin.

Also, per usual, her dad began the conversation. "Hey, Lovebug, tell me what you know about where you're going. Are you crazy excited? I've heard they have all the latest technology since Google just sponsored Presidio Prep's new think tank lab. I've also heard they handpicked an exceptional mix of genius for this particular freshman class."

She watched his hands flex on the steering wheel, excitement radiating off him. "Did you know you'll be working alongside some of the brightest minds and influencers of your age? Darren said that kids from all over the Bay Area are converging there. He said, and I quote, 'This is where Jett will learn how to change the world!'" Daddio gulped air while Mother's disbelief escaped through clenched teeth. Jett knew this from the quiet "humph" that accompanied it. She watched Daddio glance at Mother, a silent warning. He gulped one more time and cleared his throat. "On second thought, maybe I should go back to school and you can take over the law practice. What do you say, kiddo?"

Jett saw him watching her in the rearview mirror. She smiled as she shook her head. Daddio was always joking like that, and it put Jett at ease to hear his enthusiasm. Darren, her quasi-uncle, was his law partner, and they were quite a dynamic team.

But just like that, Mother interrupted the moment. Jett was ready. She pulled out her phone to take notes, knowing Mother would have a laundry list of things to consider.

"What I want to know, Jett, is who do you want to be? And what do you need to do, to be who you want to be?"

To pin Jett with her eyes, she turned around fully. "Have you done all the requisite prework? Do you have your assignments? Are you feeling ready? This is a big deal, you know, but no pressure. A lot of high-profile parents send their children here to learn how to make their mark. I'm just expecting you to make it through. And if you try really hard? You might even fit in and make friends. But you're going to have to try, Jett—really, really try!"

Jett dropped her phone in her lap. She furrowed her brow, trying to process mounting evidence that reinforced Mother's belief she wasn't normal. Jett blinked rapidly. How did Mother *do* that, just casually peel away another layer of tender confidence? She pulled her backpack tighter to herself and stared out the window, trying not to let Mother's anxiety sink into her skin.

Mother prattled on. "I'm sure you'll get the hang of the academics, but also watch and learn from the kids who are succeeding in all the things. I'm sure you can figure out who to look to for an example, who to be friends with, right? If not, my friends and colleagues have offered to help you. Any one of them will make time for you. Amy, in particular, does a lot of work with girls your age. Plus she gave an amazing keynote address at the Child and Adolescent Psychology conference in Toronto. Did you know her TED Talk has reached 58 million views? Say the word and I'll make you an appointment. You have *options,* so you can be who you want to be."

Trying to disappear, Jett sank further into her seat. Mother's eyes focused on her; from under her lowered gaze, Jett spied Mother's self-congratulatory smile. She tried to not internalize the delivery, to sort out the meaning instead of the message. Mother really wasn't the bad guy. She wasn't! So why then did she leave Jett feeling so inept, so worthless?

Her mind kept racing back. *She's not normal.* Jett wondered how her own mother could be so blind. Exactly what had she done to make Mother lose confidence in her abilities? What series of actions warranted such a painful hypothesis? And, given her bias, what could Jett do now to prove Mother wrong, to prove she was normal, just like she always knew she was?

Who did she want to be? Jett wanted to be herself – her normal, engaged, comfortable, Self, of course. But how did she say that to someone who wasn't listening?

As they crossed the Golden Gate Bridge, Jett picked up her phone again. She typed in some notes, including *"learn how to better replicate the most successful peers."* She knew Mother was staring at her, waiting for a response, but Jett just couldn't. She didn't have it in her to defend herself, to admit she had listened to her parents' private conversation, to dispute the painful reality spilling from her mother.

That settled it. Time to move forward. Jett straightened her shoulders. After all, the cursory research from earlier that morning *did* support Jett's experience over Mother's theory. Jett knew what she had to do, if not exactly how to do it. She would just have to prove Mother wrong. And a high school full of incredibly bright, promising peers seemed just the right place to shine.

As they slowed to a stop in front of Presidio Prep, Jett looked out the car window. Daddio twisted around to try to catch her eye.

"Bug, you have everything you need, right? It's probably not cool for me to take a picture of you on your first day of school anymore, but don't be too surprised if I do. Your old man thinks this day deserves documentation." Daddio's grin was so warm and encouraging, Jett felt it more than saw it.

She grinned back.

"Jett, you can do this," said Mother. "Just take notes on anything that doesn't make sense. We can go over it tonight, okay? If you need something urgently, call or text. I'll make myself available."

Jett nodded once. Her smile faded even though she knew Mother had good intentions. She was trying to be supportive.

Mother reached towards her, but Jett was faster. She opened her door and sprang out of the car. She had arrived.

"See you later."

Jett charged up the stairs of her new school, sure of success. What could go wrong?

Just looking around gave her a thrill. From the red tiled roofs above milky-white stucco to the red brick buildings nearby, Jett wondered if all her haunts would be punctuated by shades of red. And as she looked out at the Golden Gate Bridge spanning the San Francisco Bay, she felt her heart leap. What a site to inspire learning. She loved old buildings with new uses. She loved rolling lawns of green, the iconic Golden Gate Bridge and her deep blue bay. This place was amazing! And this year was also going to be amazing. She could feel it in her bones.

Jett pulled out her phone to study the campus map and find her Foundations class. Here it was, but the room looked empty and dark. She realized she was early and settled in next to the locked door. As she leaned against the wall, her pack drooped and she sighed.

This wasn't the first time; Jett liked to be early. The teacher would probably open up the classroom soon, and Jett would have first pick of seats. Yay! She had time to muse.

Apparently Presidio Prep called social studies "Foundations." Jett smirked. Shouldn't something important, something actually foundational, like math or science or *something* academic, be Foundations? Why social studies?

Thirteen people passed Jett in the hall, four pairs of two, one group of four and a singleton. She overheard an upperclassman talking to a younger student. "Yeah, you've got it good. Diaz is a cool teacher, and since she leads your Foundations team for all four years? You're gonna have fun!"

Jett snorted. She couldn't help it. But still, she tried to hide it by folding over herself to retie her shoe. *See?* she thought. They'd just proved her point. How was fun important? Foundational? Ha! Maybe the students weren't so bright if they needed four years of the same class. It sounded like a tedious waste of time.

Jett watched a man wearing a khaki colored uniform approach her classroom. Except for his big ring of keys, he looked the same as all the other national park maintenance staff, well-kept and practical. Was he also a janitor or building manager or something? She stared curiously as he unlocked the classroom, flipped on the lights, and left, without ever saying a word.

Now that her classroom was unlocked, what was the protocol here? Should she go in? Ensure she secured the spot she wanted? Or wait? Shouldn't the teacher enter first? That's what used to happen at her old school. Jett hoisted up her pack but didn't make a move to enter.

She went on to think about the protocol of assignments. Even the pre-class assignment was dumb. Jett couldn't believe the teacher had actually assigned a personal essay on love. Was Ms. Diaz trying to be cool by assigning something teenagers were supposed to be interested in?

Jett shook her head. Research had led her down many paths, and it had been difficult to sort out precisely what to include. She hadn't enjoyed the project, and that was a first for her. Researching *love* had turned out to be a monumental task.

But she had her paper, and she had done a thorough job putting it together.

Jett suspected the academics here would not challenge her, but she wouldn't tell her parents that. Already they were too divided on whether she should go to this elite magnet school instead of one closer to home. She wanted to be here, among other high achievers. Her old school was considered very good but still, she hadn't ever experienced that before. This could take learning to a whole new level; the possibilities were electrifying.

Jett watched as two classmates approached. Both looked familiar, but she couldn't place them. She knew she should recognize them even though they hadn't met. Strangers who looked familiar but weren't? That always confounded her. She kept staring.

The two were so engaged in catching up that neither saw her. Jett knew it. Neither saw the girl in cuffed Levi's and an oversized shirt, waiting by the classroom. They started for the door, and Jett moved to follow.

"I loved your latest content, Linda. Are you going to share about our life at this new school?" The boy held the door open while waiting for a response.

"Thanks, Carlos. I was thinking…"

Jett didn't hear the girl's reply as the door slammed in her face.

What? Did they not even see her? She looked around, but no one else seemed to notice her either. Shocked, Jett looked down and reconsidered her choice of outfits. She wanted to blend in with *peers*, not with the wall! She waited a moment before following them into the classroom.

As she entered, Jett took a step back. Dang! She knew who these two were. Mother was always trying to get her to track social media, pop culture, and stuff. She was pretty sure that was Carlos Rodriguez and Ruby Steffano!

Carlos looked like the soccer prodigy and popular Latin heartthrob. He was even wearing a team jersey. It might be him—could be, probably was. Huh.

And the very fair redhead next to him? The one he called Linda? She looked like the "Ruby" Mother wanted her to follow, the one with fourteen million followers and constant press. She had the same mannerisms as the ones Jett observed on Mother's phone. Mother would be so excited.

Jett wasn't. She shrugged and thought, *This should be entertaining.* They had Foundations together for the next four years—a soccer prodigy, a teen media mogul, and Jett. And, if these were leaders? Hmph. She rolled her eyes.

Jett chose a seat about halfway back, not the "try hard" section in the front nor the "rebel" section in the back. As other students filed in, she couldn't help but watch the drama playing out in front of her. Carlos continued to seek the spotlight.

"Did you see my last practice?" he asked too loudly.

She wondered if he knew who he was talking to. Carlos Rodriguez may be a soccer prodigy, but that was Ruby Steffano, virtual influencer and reigning Queen of Teen Culture. Her name definitely was not Linda. Hmm. Jett wrote another note on her phone and wondered if she should let someone know about his mistake. Maybe he had a traumatic brain injury?

She studied Ruby. Her mother would call the way Ruby was sitting a power pose. Would Ruby rip him apart for getting her name wrong? Jett knew how she would respond. But how would Ruby? She seemed like a different species altogether.

"Carlos, you player, you know I was there." A smile slid across Ruby's face. "You only missed a ball when you were staring my way." With raised eyebrows and a smirk on her pouty lips, she tossed her stylish hair and glanced around. "How could I forget? How could anyone forget?" Muffled laughter surrounded them, but Carlos didn't seem to mind. He just shrugged and with color rising on the back of his neck, eyes twinkling, he smiled at her.

Jett stared in fascination as the class filled. *Interesting...* Ruby didn't react as Jett had expected, but neither had Carlos. Ruby wasn't loud or mean, really. She didn't confront him about getting her name wrong, and

Carlos didn't seem to mind the possible dig about missing the ball. Was he a talented actor, even with a TBI? Or did he really not mind? Huh. How surprising. Was this the kind of thing Mother wanted her to learn?

She looked around. She couldn't find a common denominator. Each peer seemed unique and, in that, the same. A tall and gangly Indian boy that reminded Jett of a giraffe sat to her right. A striking girl with ebony skin sat to her left—a sleek black cat.

Ruby sat directly in front of her with Carlos to her right. Jett thought of Sally from *Cars* and El Chupacabra from *Planes*.

She shook her head. Obviously, her movies list needed an update. Maybe she could find favorites that weren't animal documentaries or cartoons? Jett put a note in her phone to research popular teen movies.

Someone threw the classroom door open wide. A diminutive Latina woman in bright, happy tones strode up to the big desk and dropped her things into the teacher's seat. Her grin was bright enough to light the farthest corners of the room.

"Good morning, fresh. I am Ms. Diaz. We'll be building foundations together for the next four years, and I am so pleased you are here! To quote one of my favorite movies, 'This class is social studies. That is, you and the world.' Does anyone know this reference? Extra points if you can name the character who said it, in what film, and the year it came out. Hint: It was before you were born." No hands were raised, and Jett sighed in relief. Another sign she was normal. No one knew the movie this teacher had referred to.

"Anyone? Anyone? Anyone?" said the teacher to a silent student body. She shook her head. "Oh, come on, fresh! Be so! I want you engaged. I want you *involved*, and most of all, I want you to sort out society and how you fit! You all fail at teen movie trivia, by the way. I expect better. Be fresh, but learn from the past.

"Let's try this again. Maybe something more current? Who knows the chorus to 'My Shot?'" Ms. Diaz looked around and clapped in delight.

"Good! Well that's most of you then. Join me?"

The teacher lowered her voice, cupped her hands around her mouth, and began a rhythmic cadence. Jett searched the faces of those nearby, noting their reactions. Was she the only one who thought Ms. Diaz was weird? It just might be. Many of her peers had joined this crazy person who was supposedly a teacher. They were all chanting.... something. Huh. What was she missing?.

Nodding her appreciation to those in the know, Ms. Diaz beamed four thousand watts of enthusiasm. "Good! Now those of you who joined in, teach the others. Make your core group of... five. Start pairing up with those near you. I expect a rousing chorus in"—the teacher looked at her watch—"twenty minutes. This is a contest and you will be graded."

What? Jett tensed. She looked around. How was this going to...?

"Hey, you! Wake up. You're in our Core5. And I think you're the only one who doesn't know it. So we're good and you'll just have to catch up. You gotta brain?" snapped Ruby. She looked Jett over critically and a nasty smile lit her entire face when she saw Jett's backpack. She sighed, shook her head, and still laughing to herself, dismissed Jett. "Maybe not," Ruby mumbled.

Jett thought, *That's okay. I dismissed you an hour ago.*

"How's your memory? Can you remember things?" asked Carlos. That was ironic considering his faulty memory and calling Ruby "Linda."

The sleek black cat purred, "Okay then... This is awkward. I'm Sam." Sam looked at the others in her group. "Gather up. We're gonna add in some freestyle."

Sam seemed okay, but what was freestyle? Jett was sure everyone else knew. Too bad she couldn't risk asking. That would totally *not* be normal.

"I'm Andy," said the giraffe, the only other boy in the group besides Carlos.

Jett looked toward the ground when he spoke. *Huh. He has crazy socks. This Andy guy is actually a character. Wonder if he'll be smarter than Ruby or Carlos?*

"Gather in tight so no one overhears. We don't want anyone to steal our greatness. Let's do this!" Carlos added.

Her Core5 huddled closer. Jett felt crowded. At least she knew some names now. Everyone else seemed to know what was expected. Jett had to learn quickly. At least that was normal for her.

Pretty soon she was immersed in learning the popular verse and some form of dance moves termed freestyle, whatever that meant. It didn't look very cohesive or coordinated. Jett surreptitiously searched for it on her phone and felt better. She could dance her own style while they each did the same. Time flew by and suddenly it was their turn to get up in front of the rest of the class. Jett found it interesting how her classmates didn't hold back for fear of judgment. They were all in. They knew the words. They knew their own movement. They performed with pitch and passion. Jett just tried to do what they were doing and in a timely manner, hoping no one caught on to her slight delay. Looked to her like they didn't. *Phew!* Jett's group won applause, hoots, and hollers.

She had been so immersed in trying to learn what her group already knew that she didn't have time to ask before. Now she did. She took out her phone to take down a note to research this poem. "Just so I'm clear, what was that?"

Suddenly the rest of the class was laughing at her, not with her. She could tell. She wasn't laughing. Going from the smartest one in school to the punchline of a joke was inconceivable, yet here she was. And for the first time, Jett felt like a misfit. She saw it as everyone else shared in the laugh she didn't understand. And at that moment? She hated them all.

"Now, now," scolded Ms. Diaz. Jett watched carefully as the teacher tried to compose herself. She took a breath and tried again. "Are you willing to throw away *your* shot just because someone asked a question you deemed rudimentary? One of your own, by the way. Is that the kind of society we desire to be? And, while sorting through our collective cruelty, you can all return to your seats. I'm including myself in the collective because I smiled, but it really wasn't funny and I'm kind of done with this."

The class went silent as they found their spots.

But Ms. Diaz really wasn't done. She pinned many with her laser-like gaze. "Mmm-hm, I thought so. Who here has their personal essay on love? Any one of you want to expand on that for us? Obviously it wasn't something you thought deeply about. Please turn it in. And, to answer your question, Ms. ... ?"

Eyes downcast, Jett didn't know she was being addressed. Then all eyes were on her and she couldn't look up; there was too much weight in that many stares. The quiet grew expectant.

When the silence stretched too long and no one answered, no one even moved, Jett forced herself to raise her eyes. Looking around she found not only the teacher but also most of the class still staring at her.

Ms. Diaz repeated herself. "Ms. ... ?"

The heat of embarrassment creeped up Jett's neck. "Harper. Ms. Jett Harper."

"Ah! Thank you, Ms. Harper. To answer your question: That little bit was extracted from a musical by Lin-Manuel Miranda called *Hamilton*." Ms. Diaz looked around. "Your papers, class, are they all in? Good!" After collecting Jett's too, she laid them on top of her desk and looked up.

"Now, in case you didn't know, our school, our intellectual playground as it were, can also be seen as a forward-reaching rebel think tank, striving to produce sustainable leadership with moxie and manners. Does that sound like you?" She waited for a response, but no one volunteered. She continued. "That definition was created by last year's graduating class. Each Foundations class has their own message to mentor, one that is created and honed by your fourth year. This class obviously needs to start with the basics, and that little drama convinced me we're right on track. I've decided we will build our Foundation on love. Objections? No? Good!" She looked around again.

No response.

"Anyone dare to share more about *Hamilton* and their opinion on why it matters today?"

Finally, hands shot up. As the class focus redirected, Jett relaxed. Academics. *Yay*! She could do this. The environment might be a bit progressive, but she could... Her thoughts were interrupted. Oh no. She'd missed something and she was caught, in front of everyone.

"Ms. Harper, are you with us? Care to share what thoughts are filling your head? You count too, and I want to hear from you. Will you be part of our social studies experiment?"

Jett nodded and refocused.

"As I was explaining, we will be creating competing projects for the freshman faire, based on our theme of love, in your new family group, your Core5. It's worth 75 percent of your grade, so get to know them and learn how to work together. The winner of the freshman faire will have their project immortalized, and the group picture will hang in the Hall of Fame. Plus you'll get a free pass on all finals for your freshman year. A team from my class has won the last five times. I expect us to win this year as well. Any questions?"

Hands again shot up around the room, and Jett's heart sank. Her "Core5" might have worked with her to learn the *Hamilton* lyrics quickly, but she knew from experience she would be carrying them through this project. She hated group projects because she hated giving away her work for free so that others could get the same grade as her. That had been her experience every single time.

So much for a new school with new possibilities. How did the teacher not understand the dynamics of collaborative projects? Was it Jett's place to teach the teacher? What about when the inequity of this model was so evident? What about when their ignorance impacted her performance?

She had been down this road before, and she didn't want to make waves if it would affect her grade or her ability to prove herself. She knew what she would do, and most likely it wouldn't involve teaching the teacher. She would work. They would watch. Sometimes someone might assist if she asked and if they even got what she was asking them to do, but in any case, history had proven she would work and they all would share her grade. And she would pass on top marks to Carlos with his TBI, to sparkly influencer Ruby, and to the other two less-offensive members of her team. That's what she had to do to get what she needed.

Was it worth it? She looked around again. Did she want to share her top marks with Ruby and Carlos? No! The other two flanking her? Maybe. All she knew was she had to get the grade, and lucky for them, they would come along. And that was Jett's normal. Not her preference, but what she knew. By the time class was over, she was annoyed but resigned. She took out her phone again. New note to self: *Take Core5 all the way to freshman faire and win.*

DAY ONE: COMPLETE. Yay! As much as she was excited to begin high school, Jett was glad to be home. Who knew it would be so exhausting?

She set down her backpack and started making the perfect after-school snack: microwave popcorn. While her treat was popping, she wondered what to do with her afternoon. So far, no classes had assigned homework, but she was still driven to make progress. In Jett's mind, popcorn meant movies. How could she justify watching movies instead of working? Maybe she could consider this a research party? Jett wanted to ace Mother's assignments, too. If she watched and analyzed examples of successful teens in action, she could also update her movie references, and improve her pop culture knowledge. This would be an excellent use of free time. Potentially this one activity took two tasks off her to-do list!

Another idea, possibly brilliant, popped into her head: Crime Shows. On most of the ones she'd seen, they had these walls of data—clues—all visible together, so they could sort out the relationship and solve the mystery. Could she build one? Maybe? She could certainly try. Jett would put up all the information she gathered, find the threads holding each fact together, and weave them into a pattern, resolving her hypothesis. Yeah! *That!* Now she was even more excited to knuckle down and get to work. Channeling her inner detective, she would put all she'd learned about being a popular teen up on one wall for easy access.

Excited, she sprinted into the office. With just a little hunting, she unearthed an unused corkboard, a box of pins, and a stack of index cards. She already had a complete set of colored pens in her Spiketus Rex. She carried her supplies into the family room and set them down next to her popcorn bowl.

She grabbed her phone, looked up the top movies for teens, and found many differing opinions. But one movie made almost every list. It was old, but so what? So was Daddio, and he was still cool. Jett started with *The Breakfast Club,* pulled out a stack of note cards, and got to work.

Jett listened. She watched. She took notes. Pressed pause. Thought. Rewound and took more notes. "You see us as a Brain, an Athlete, a Basket Case, a Princess, and a Criminal." And just like that, the story line stole Jett away.

The movie transported her into moments as if they were happening to her, not on a screen in front of her.

And then, quite suddenly, she heard strange noises outside her window. Dragged out of the story and dropped back into her living room, Jett shook her head to clear the displacement. Gah! What was going on out there?

Having lost sight of her story analysis and character data, she went to investigate. First, though, she took the few notecards she had started and stacked them on the board. She would have to rewind and begin again where the story had swallowed her whole. That is, after she sorted the sounds outside. They were still going on. Jett began to worry. In her neighborhood, commotions rarely lasted so long. What could it be?

Now-empty popcorn bowl in hand, she took it to the kitchen sink and rinsed it, then drifted outside—and stopped. She stood on her front porch, transfixed. Jett rubbed her eyes. She couldn't believe it.

Really? It looked like her neighbor from down the street was playing with a puppy and they were headed her way. A gangly, grinning, caramel-colored, floppy-tongued fuzz ball looked up at her. And she couldn't help but grin back.

"Well, who's this?" mused the man trying to keep up with the curious puppy.

Jett looked over as she walked down her front stairs. "Hello, sir. I'm Jett Harper and this is my house. Who are you?"

"Oh my! Such manners for one so young. It is a pleasure to make your acquaintance, Ms. Harper. I am Benjamin Calbert-Otto. You are welcome to call me Ben. And my house is just down the block."

She'd thought he looked familiar. He must be that new guy who'd moved into Jenny Owens' home. Mother had said he was uniquely singular. But she was wrong: he had a dog.

Ben looked at the puppy busily sniffing Jett's pant leg. "This is my pup for the next little while. After that he'll either go back to school so he can learn to be a service dog or a really good family dog. Do you think he'll graduate from his school?"

"Hmmm, I don't know. What does he have to learn?"

The puppy was currently tugging on her pant leg, trying to engage her in his games.

Ben shrugged his shoulders. "I don't know, little miss. I just know right now he has to learn his manners. Once he knows what's expected, I'll need to see whether he reacts particularly strongly to anything or if he stays focused. Is he silly or stable? You know, things like that. I am taking notes," Ben explained, holding up his phone. "I'm just part of his manners training."

Jett nodded slowly, taking in all the information. She looked down at the playful pup. "I think he's silly. What's his name?" Even though he was younger than her parents, Jett also thought Ben must be a full-grown adult. He had a lot of responsibility, ensuring the puppy had manners *and* documenting the progress.

Ben watched the puppy smell a tree. "I don't know. He doesn't really have one yet."

"*What?*" Jett exploded. "I'm sorry. I'm sure I missed something. Did you just admit he doesn't have a name?" She waited for a correction, but Ben just nodded. Jett's face screwed up with confusion. "I don't understand. How can this be? What do you call him? How do you get him to follow you?"

This made no sense. Before her stood her neighbor, who, undeniably, was an adult. Was he capable? Competent? He certainly was not normal. Is that what Mother feared for her? That she wouldn't know the importance of taking care of details?

Ben smiled patiently. "I just whistle, and he comes over. Watch." Ben whistled, and the pup with no name came bounding over. He sat and looked up at Ben expectantly. He reached down to pet the waiting pup.

"I don't… I don't… " Jett stammered. She shook her head. "I don't… " She sighed and tried again. "He needs a *name*." And Ben needed his guardianship revoked if he didn't understand the importance of names.

Ben smiled again and quoted Shakespeare. "A rose by any other name would smell as sweet."

Jett shook her head in exasperation. Why did grown-ups do that? Why did they quote something abstract to support faulty logic?

"Yes, yes. Shakespeare. Juliet says that phrase in lines 43–44, act 2, scene 2 of *Romeo and Juliet*."

Pacing back and forth, she clasped her hands tightly behind her back, trying to restrain all the thoughts running straight through her head to her mouth. Jett wanted to be polite, which meant not overwhelming an adult with too much information. That usually happened when she skipped the crucial step of assessing a new acquaintance's cognitive ability.

She wanted to give him the benefit of the doubt as Daddio had taught her to do, innocent until proven guilty and all that. But they'd entrusted this man with a living being, and he was not fulfilling basic obligations such as giving the dog a name. She wanted to be open as Mother would have required. She wanted to "be curious as to the why," but it was too much. Jett lost the struggle. She held nothing back.

"Do you have any idea how hard it would be to understand who is supposed to do what when you don't know how to differentiate yourself as a who? Can you imagine being so inconsequential as to not be given a name? Do you know *Star Trek: The Next Generation*? My parents said I need to ask new people this because not everyone is smart enough to watch *Star Trek*. But you seem smart, so do you think this pup is a Borg or something? Borgs aren't really real, by the way. He's not an alien. He's a puppy. And this pup needs a name. You need to fix this, Ben. How can you be a responsible grown-up, an *adult*, and not see this?" She was fidgeting again.

Right hand twirling in anxiety and frustration, she walked away. When at the top of her front porch, just before entering the front door, she turned around. And, with his mouth opening and closing like that, Jett thought Ben looked like a fish. She made a mental note to learn why fish opened and closed their mouths in rapid succession.

"By the way, Mr. Ben. A rose by any other name? *It still has a name!*"

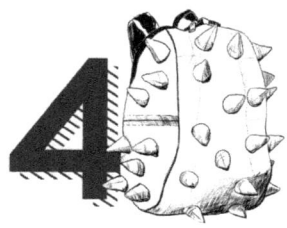

4

HALFWAY THROUGH THE Foundations class period, Ms. Diaz returned graded assignments. Finally! Had it really been two weeks since the school year started?

Jett peeked at her neighbors to see what was being returned. It looked like the papers they'd turned in on the first day of school. The same day they'd laughed at her for asking about the quote from *Hamilton*. Well, no one would laugh at her now. She would get a top mark and start revealing her place in this class. Could she do that without smirking?

Jett had wondered how long it would take to get grades to start tracking and stacking. Sam was grinning. Good. And Andy was grinning. Also a good sign. He must have done all right too. They might be decent teammates on that infernal group project.

Jett liked Andy's manners. He was quiet and unassuming but when he spoke, it was powerful. Was it because he had something to say rather than just speaking because he wanted to hear his own voice? He was not loud and proud like Carlos nor blindingly bright and sparkly like Ruby. Jett liked that about him. Plus he wore outrageous socks. Jett peeked every day to see what he would be sporting. Today's socks had dog faces all over them, kind of like polka dots but dog faces. She wondered if anyone else had noticed his socks.

As she looked around, Jett noted that all the other students seemed to be pleased. Many of her peers were smiling, giving each other high fives and otherwise celebrating. Huh. Good news then for everyone? Huh. Curious and ready to receive her A, Jett waited for her paper to be returned. Maybe she would receive extra credit for her exceptional research skills.

Ms. Diaz walked up to her. She handed Jett a paper, but it sported no letter grade on it. It wasn't even her paper returned. Where was her work? This paper was practically blank, all except for her name neatly printed in the top right-hand corner and the See Me note signed by Ms. Diaz in the middle of the page. Jett started to bounce.

She had expected her work to be well received, but this well? Oh my. She couldn't sit still. Trying to process the news, Jett decided the teacher didn't want to be perceived as showing favoritism to her by recognizing the remarkable quality of her work in front of the entire class just yet. This was only getting better. She wondered what accolades awaited her. She could barely sit still as she waited for class to end.

As she waited, she continued to compose her argument about abolishing the unfair practice of group projects. While she wouldn't mind working alongside Andy and maybe Sam, Carlos shouldn't be asked to do the same level of work, what with his traumatic brain injury. Ruby, on the other hand, was smart in her own right but also super-entitled and elitist. From their few interactions and all observations thus far, she was sure Ruby expected to sign her name to the group project and call that an actual contribution. She was also sure Ruby would expect the team to be grateful for her endorsement or some such drivel. Jett fumed just thinking about it. A huff escaped her body. Obviously, Ruby acted as if fame and fortune meant she could delegate anything she didn't see as deserving of her time—including schoolwork. Ruby might have been some type of leader/influencer, but she clearly was not a team player.

And Carlos? That athlete was just... Well, it was sad, really. He walked around like the king of the world, and people treated him as such. He was a stereotypical example of the outrageously popular athletes who had everything handed to them just because they were good with a ball. Why did sports matter so much? Is that where he'd gotten hurt and lost his brain capacity? It was possible, maybe even probable. Was his injury public knowledge and she just hadn't heard yet? Maybe that was why everyone followed his lead. Jett made herself a note to Google him and see if she could sort out who knew about his TBI. Yes, she definitely had to explain to the teacher why group projects just weren't fair.

The bell sounded, and instead of rushing to her next class, Jett hung back.

"Hi, Jett. Looks like you got my note. Are you ready to talk about your paper, or did you want to schedule a better time?"

"I can spare a moment now if you can make it work. I'm excited to get my paper back and hear your thoughts."

Her teacher frowned. "Are you sure, Jett? Why don't we handle this at lunchtime?"

"Really? You're going to keep me in suspense?" Jett started rocking back and forth, up and down, on the balls of her feet.

"Um, no," Ms. Diaz said, frowning. "We can do this now if you really want to."

Jett nodded emphatically. "I'm sure. I don't want to wait."

"Okay. Please sit down. I'm thinking we're not on the same page here."

Jett sat, hands in her lap but bursting with energy. She rolled her wrists, subtly trying to dispel the extra tension built up in her excitement. Yay for doing this now and yay for this being an empty classroom so she could learn the good news. But how would Ms. Diaz handle her protest of group projects?

Ms. Diaz slowly withdrew Jett's paper from her desk drawer. "Jett, I don't know why you didn't do the assignment as requested."

Jett frowned.

"I assigned a personal essay on love so I could get to know you and how you see this important topic, how you connect to society through this lens."

"Ms. Diaz, I assure you this is personal. This *is* my essay on love, complete with hypothesis and supporting arguments. I did not plagiarize, although I expect you aren't used to freshman papers of this caliber. That would be a simple mistake to make."

The teacher raised her hand to interrupt Jett's interruption. "Jett, that is not what I was implying." She handed the paper back.

Jett looked down at the paper now in her hands. There was a big red letter A, but it was missing the right side... There was a... There was a... Jett squinted. What? She looked up in utter and complete shock. She was glad she was sitting down.

Jett tried to refocus on what her teacher was saying. "Excuse me? I seem to have missed something."

Ms. Diaz nodded. "Yes, Jett. I think you did. I think maybe you are still missing something. Can you take a few deep breaths please?"

Jett couldn't stop staring at the right side of the A, which was missing the downward line. That made it look like an F.

Inconceivable! Who did this teacher think she was? Jett *personally* wrote an essay on love. It was a *personal* essay. How could Ms. Diaz think *she* was missing something?

Maybe the teacher was. Jett looked around the room, trying to gather evidence for her latest theory, but she simply didn't know the teacher well enough yet.

"Excuse me, Ms. Diaz. I know this is your class and all. I know I am to learn from you for the next four years. I know you probably have a really good, maybe even logical, reason for your misinterpretation. But I just cannot let this go unchallenged. You dye your hair. Your hair is really white. What is your age? Do you live alone? Are you feeling lonely or depressed? Does someone at home make sure you eat? Maybe you forget to drink water or other beverages. You wear glasses. Do you also have a problem hearing? Do you know where your keys are? Who is the president? Maybe you have dementia? Did you know Carlos probably has a TBI? He is showing obvious symptoms. For example, he calls Ruby "Linda"! And I think she knows he has brain damage, too, because she never challenges him." Jett was nodding her head as she spoke and watching Ms. Diaz very carefully to assess her reactions.

The teacher's facial expressions went from shocked to affronted to smirking and finally to barely stifling her laughter. "Oh Jett, you *are* going to challenge me, aren't you?" she sighed. "Okay. Here's the thing. I like you. You bring so much—such a new perspective for me to consider. I'm going to cut you a break if you'll take on this challenge. And you can check—I rarely offer second chances. Are you interested in hearing me out?"

Jett sat there, silent. Realizing the teacher was waiting for a response, she gave a curt nod. She would listen. She knew society expected her to listen to authority figures even when they weren't as smart as her. They held the power after all. That reminded her of her sound argument against group projects. Maybe she *would* have to teach this teacher. She sighed audibly and looked up.

"If I had asked for a research paper, you would have received an A."

Jett nodded. That made sense.

"It's obvious you know how to work. Your Core5 will appreciate that. But you didn't give me the assignment I asked for. They won't appreciate your work if you don't work with them on the actual project. I asked for a personal essay, meaning a paper solely about how *you* experience love. You didn't do that. But you can make up for it tonight."

Jett tilted her head, confused. None of this made sense.

"If you go home and write me a paper about how *you* experience love, I'll read it and grade it. Right now, because of this paper, you are on academic probation. You will remain so until your grades improve enough to erase this one, or until you replace it with your new paper. The new one will need to be graded C or better. Either way, I will need a signature from either your parents or the academic counselor acknowledging this failed assignment. Take this paper home for your parents to sign or take it to Mr. Williams, who can also sign it for you. He will require an appointment with you but will also look after you academically. It's usually best to make him aware of students who aren't up to assignments right as they happen. I'm sure you know this from past assignments though, right?"

All the muscles in Jett's body tensed, and she started to shake from the effort to process the unthinkable. Her eyes burned with the effort to hold on to hot tears. She was overloading. This still didn't make sense to her. She *didn't* know. She had only ever received top marks in school. And her first assignment in high school received a... Had gotten a... She was on... Jett didn't want her parents to know she'd failed, and she didn't want to see a counselor, even just an academic one. She didn't. She couldn't. This didn't—her brain was short-circuiting.

"Jett? Jett? Take a deep breath. Okay. Good. Again. Now tell me what you want to do." Startled at the sound of the bell, Ms. Diaz jumped. "Oh my. Okay. We've taken up more time than I expected. I'll write a note for you to take to the office. I guess you can think about it, and if you turn in a fresh paper, I'll know your answer." Ms. Diaz handed Jett a piece of paper. "Here. Time to go. We both need to get ready for the next class."

Jett just sat there. Numb. Mute. Not moving.

"Jett? Seriously. Time to go. You'll be off academic probation if you turn in the assignment I asked for, make an average grade, and get the signature. Easy-peasy. You can do this. Just write it. Get the old one signed and I'll see you tomorrow, okay?"

Jett stood up and nodded. Okay. She had heard Ms. Diaz. She just didn't know how she was supposed to write a better paper in one night. She didn't know what she didn't know. And this time she didn't know where to find an answer, either. What she did know, clearly, was she could not remain on academic probation and she could not let her parents know she'd failed. That certainly wasn't normal.

Deep breath was right.

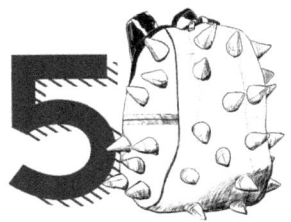

EVEN AS SHE rounded the corner on her home block, Jett's mind remained at school. She tried to wrap her brain around all that had happened. She couldn't. Her head kept spinning around this new reality. New reality and new paper, both unfathomable and not yet over. She wanted a distraction. Jett looked around.

Up ahead, she saw the puppy with no name and Mr. Calbert-Otto. She had demoted her neighbor Ben to "that man with a puppy, Mr. Calbert-Otto" after he admitted he didn't know the puppy's name. Jett reasoned this would help her remember to *try* to be respectful, since he was, technically, an adult. She was relieved to see the puppy with no name happily playing and working on his skills. She wanted to observe him a bit longer. Maybe Mr. Otto would answer a few questions for her. Could he help her understand love for her paper due tomorrow? It was time to see what he knew. She whistled, and the pup came running.

Ben looked up at Jett's whistle, "Well hello, new chum. Want some gum?" He extended a pack of gum she hadn't noticed him holding.

She wondered if it would be more polite to decline or just to hold onto it. She didn't really like gum. "Good afternoon, Mr. Otto. Thank you. How is your day proceeding?" Jett took a piece of gum and put it in her pack to discard later.

Ben tilted his head to the side and did his best fish impression again, opening and closing his mouth as if taking in air. Jett had done her research. Apparently, all fish breathed by constantly opening and closing their mouths. If Ben were a comic book character, maybe he would be Fishman or something?

Ben took a moment and then answered. "My day was proceeding with blind haste but now has slowed with caution. Mr. Otto now, huh? Tell me what's going on, young Data."

It was Jett's turn to tilt her head. Did Mr. Otto just make a *Star Trek: The Next Generation* reference? Data was her favorite character. She nodded once in acknowledgement as she accepted the compliment. The puppy was still sitting at attention in front of her, looking up for a clue on the next part of this game. Jett smiled as she looked down. Pup with no name started wagging his tail. She signaled him for a round of puppy pushups, something she learned from observing Ben earlier, and returned her focus to him.

"I have a serious inquiry and your response would greatly help my knowledge base. Are you willing to help me?"

Ben stared at her. "Um, this is intriguing, but I cannot tell you if I will be of help when you have yet to ask me your questions. I *can* promise you can ask me, and I will tell you no lies."

Jett now nodded several times and gestured for the pup to circle around her. "Thank you. That would be helpful. I need to learn about love. What can you tell me?"

Again, her neighbor looked like a fish who needed to breathe. "Well, I can tell you love is … love can be … " He puffed his cheeks like a lionfish. "Okay, love is a feeling, expressed by actions that uplift both the giver and the recipient. Do you need to know more?"

Jett nodded insistently. "Yes, Mr. Otto. I need to know a whole lot more. I need something personal. Tell me about how you experience love."

"Huh?!? What? I'm sorry, friend, but I don't kiss and tell. I'm not that kind."

Jett's turn to tilt her head as she processed this. "Does kissing have to do with love?"

"Well, not always," admitted Ben. "Let's talk about another kind of love. See the pup?"

Jett nodded.

"I love him. I feed him, bathe him, play with him. I walk him, teach him, nurture him. I show him I love him by how I treat him and by how I take his needs into account."

Jett nodded slowly. "Does he love you?"

"Ah! Good question! I would say yes. He is happy to see me, listens, engages, always wants my company. I would have to say yes."

Both looked at the pup with no name who was lying down now, starting to snore.

"Does anyone else love you?"

Ben's face fell. He smiled, not full-wattage but slowly and with warmth, wattage growing as he considered. "Yes, Jett. Others love me, too. I have an entire community who loves me, including friends and family. They just don't live with me and I don't see them as much as this pup."

"Okay. Then, how do you know they love you? How do you experience love with them?"

"I know when someone does something for me, spends time with me, hugs me, gives me a gift that shows they are thinking of me. They could simply tell me, and I can hear it in their tone of voice. There are lots of ways I get love from others."

Jett was astonished. So many ways Mr. Otto experienced love from others! He must be worthy of being a first-name acquaintance after all. "Ben, what does love sound like?"

"Mm," mused Ben. "It sounds like a hug and feels like a sonnet. It's indescribably potent because when you hear love—authentic, true love—you feel it."

"Ah," sighed Jett. She had so much new information to think about. "Thank you, Ben." She looked down at the puppy napping on her feet. "One last question for today?"

Ben nodded.

"Would love be easier with a name?"

Ben looked at Jett for a long moment, thinking about her queries. "I don't know, Jett. I don't know, but I will think about it." Ben reached down and picked up his tuckered pup. He carried the pup with no name away and Jett watched them go.

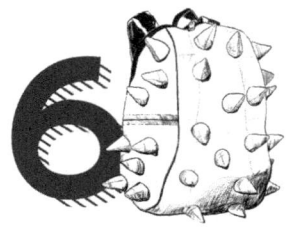

BACK IN THE family office, Jett sat down at the computer to sort more data. She looked around the room—at all the books, at the pictures, and at the art. Writing down the answers she had collected from Ben onto sticky notes, Jett wondered how her parents would answer the same questions. Not that she could ask them, of course. It was too late for that. She had told them about the initial assignment, but failed to seek their help. Asking for input now might lead them to ask questions she didn't want to answer, like, didn't she already write a paper on love? And, if so, why was she asking about it again?

Ugh. This was so arduous! So stressful. How could she write a better paper in just one night? How did she experience love? How did she know? What was love, truly, to begin with?

Jett swiveled around in the seat to face the computer and turned on a stealth browser. She didn't want anyone to be able to track her research as that, too, would bring up questions. Jett entered "how to experience love" in the search field. This differed from last time when she Googled love all by itself. Her results were—unexpected.

Jett's eyebrows rose involuntarily. Answers ran the gamut, and she took some notes, but she also was sure her teacher didn't want to hear about God or sexual partners. She hoped so, anyway. Closing the browser tabs, she opened a page to write. Jett looked at the sticky notes from Ben's answers. He experienced love in many ways, from many sources. Yet she was still at a loss. Trying to relate to Ben's experiences, Jett thought about her parents. Did they love her? They provided for her. They drove her places. Mother and Daddio expected to spend time with her in social situations. They did more than provide for her needs. They considered her desires, like her Mother hunting down clothes that were soft and without tags. Sometimes Mother even removed the tags for Jet when she couldn't find a way around that one. Yeah ... if she measured by Ben's examples, her parents loved her. What disturbed her most? Realizing that she wasn't sure she loved them back.

She flipped over her project board on teen culture and put up her notes for this project. She stood back and looked at the meager data collected. Frustrated, she decided to just write and see where it took her. Jett shook her head and began to just "rant" write.

Late in the summer before I started high school, I undertook an assignment from one of my new teachers. She asked us to write a personal paper on love. She asked that we have it with us on the first day of school, ready to turn in. I spent hours researching, processing, putting together all the relevant information about the phenomenon called love that so many obsess over. I was pleased with my work, although no closer to understanding the subject matter than before writing the paper. I still do not see why there is so much hullabaloo about something so subjective.

And maybe that is why, for the first time in my life, I flunked an assignment. This teacher was actually asking for something outside of my comprehension. Now I am to write about how I experience love. That is a foreign concept, and it baffles me that this is a requirement for my success. What if I don't experience love? Will I fail? Will I be held hostage by my lack of experience?

I asked my neighbor, and he was able to talk about his experience of love for a substantial amount of time. Apparently, he has many sources of love and many kinds to share about. I still don't get it.

What I do get is the way his face lit up when he talked about love. I heard the sparkle in his voice.

NEEDING NORMAL   51

I saw the warmth that lit his eyes. I watched his expression of love, as specified, while he played with his puppy. And yet I am no closer.

I wanted to ask my parents, but then they would wonder why, and I would have to admit my failure and the looming new assignment. Love is a foreign concept to me. I don't know if I experience it, and I have no benchmarks to quantify the how. I know this is not what my teacher wants to hear, and I am afraid I will still fail if I decide to turn in this rant, but it is my experience. My experience is that I have no experience.

Since love is a predominant theme all year long in this class, I expect I will learn more. Maybe then I won't disappoint her. Maybe then I can answer in a way that will be acceptable. I am sure I am not alone. But I don't know who else to ask about love. My research suggests love is important to many people. Maybe this year I will learn how.

Jett felt the tears on her cheeks and the speed of her heartbeat. Physiological responses to her distress. Deep breaths and count to four, Jett told herself.

Now that she had something to turn in, Jett thought about her options. If she turned it in, her teacher might think she isn't normal. Her teacher might tell her parents. Then Mother would definitely send her to counseling with

Amy or one of her other colleagues. What if they all saw the same thing? Would that same thing be what Jett saw in herself? She shook her head. Turning in this paper could be disastrous. Honestly, it could ruin her. She could turn in the paper, possibly fail again, *and* get sent to counseling.

But what about not turning it in? Jett would remain on academic probation. She would need to tell her parents and Mother would send her to Amy's ... Gah! Same outcome.

In what scenario did she get to avoid counseling offices and people assessing her well-being? In what scenario was Jett accepted as valuable, just as she was? *That* was the scenario she wanted. And the only path to that scenario meant risking ridicule, risking reassessment of her experience, and turning in a paper on how she experienced love—tomorrow!

What if she lied? What if she used the information collected from Ben and built a paper around his experience? Jett seriously considered this before remembering she had no "poker face" and couldn't pull it off if she were to be questioned—at all.

Sigh. Damn it. Gah! She was now swearing to herself, she was so upset. But really, damn it. She would just have to risk being vulnerable and turn in the rant, not a "real" paper. She would get that signature from the academic counselor, who at least wasn't a counselor like Mother or her colleagues. Fifteen minutes. She only had to give him fifteen minutes, get his signature, and turn in her rant.

Jett prayed she would just pass. For the first time ever, she just wanted to pass.

She heard the door to the kitchen open. She saw lights being turned on. Her parents were home. Time to hide this hideous embarrassment in her backpack. Jett hurried to join them before they sought her out.

7

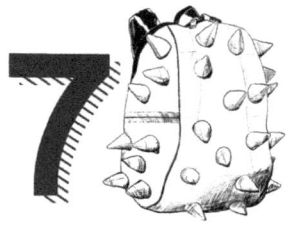

JETT WALKED INTO her Foundations class, viewing her peers through a different lens. Were they smarter than her? She felt like an imposter. Did they see her as an imposter? After all, she *was* the only one who waited after class to speak with Ms. Diaz. Did they know what happened? How would they react? She wanted to succeed, to prove her normality. Would they consider her normal if they knew about her failure?

She was nervous about turning in her rant. Jett didn't consider it a real paper and so she called it a rant, but she also knew her teacher would expect her work at some point today. She had an appointment to see that academic counselor for his signature. Today was shaping up to be an unusual day, and that bothered her. Jett loved predictability and routines. She hated unplanned anomalies, such as extra work and engaging with new people.

Thinking about what she had learned from watching, re-watching, and thoroughly studying *The Breakfast Club*, she looked at each character as an archetype, complete with distinct ways to communicate and be in this world. She wanted to apply her new knowledge. This class would be her first opportunity. She looked for her group.

Carlos was sitting at the table designated for their Core5. Wearing a rugby jersey, Carlos appeared to be interested in sports beyond soccer. From the categories she was working with, he certainly would be classified as the Athlete. Carlos smiled when he saw her looking at him.

Next to Carlos sat Ruby, busy on her phone and looking picture-perfect. Ruby was definitely a Princess. She had legions of followers and admirers. She held court every time she put her phone down. And, now that Jett thought about it, Ruby probably held court *on* her phone as well. She was the quintessential digital girl, a Princess for sure. Jett watched Ruby look at Carlos, who was inviting Jett into the mix with his smile. Ruby's eyes narrowed as she returned to her virtual court. She never even looked at Jett. She couldn't be bothered.

Involuntarily, Jett felt her tongue rolling in her mouth, pushing up against her front teeth in rapid succession and hoped no one noticed. It made her feel better, a way to dispel some pent-up energy. She kept approaching.

Both of her other teammates, Sam and Andy, were there, but they were harder to categorize. Neither seemed a Princess or an Athlete, but neither did they seem a Basket Case or a Brain. Was Sam some kind of criminal? Surely not. A Rebel or a Troublemaker? Maybe. What about Andy? Why was she sure he was not a Troublemaker? Was it his quiet, peaceful manner? Weren't his wild socks a kind of rebellion? That hardly seemed right. Jett thought about prejudice and bias, and realized she didn't have enough data yet to categorize either Andy or Sam. She *did* consider herself a Brain. Were they as well? She knew they did well on the paper she had failed. Could they actually be better at school than she was?

Jett shook her head to dislodge the uncomfortable thought. If they were the Brains, was she the Basket Case? Who was the Troublemaker? The Rebel? The tempo of her tongue crashing into her teeth increased. She would just have to look for clues to their archetypes.

"Hey, Jett, right?" asked Andy. Jett was studying his socks, though it looked like she was studying the floor. She nodded without meeting his gaze. Andy looked to Sam. Jett surreptitiously watched the silent discussion between Andy and Sam. It was all eyebrows and head tilts. She wondered what she was missing. "Yeah, well," continued Andy. "Um, I'm sure you got a good grade on the initial assignment too, so cheer up. This group project will be an easy A."

Jett's back stiffened, like someone had hit her with a stick, and she looked up. Did they not know? She wouldn't be able to carry everyone else's work on this. She *failed*. How could she keep this a secret?

Sam jumped in. "We were just going to talk about how to slay this beast. You ready?" Sam motioned to the empty seat. Jett noticed Sam was the only one sitting on the back of her chair, feet firmly planted on the seat. Maybe she was a Rebel. Jett could imagine casting Sam as a Rebel just from this one posture. Was that enough of a clue?

Her arrival seemed to have triggered the start of group discussion, and Ruby put away her phone with a heavy sigh. Sam watched. Carlos beamed. Andy opened his notebook, ready to begin.

"Who's in charge here?" Ruby demanded. "I mean, seriously, who is going to be the face of this work? You know, do the presentations and lead our group, especially at the Freshmen Faire?"

"Linda, you! You are the face!" Volunteered Carlos, but as he looked around the group for confirmation, his enthusiasm faltered. "Right?"

Sam rolled her eyes. "Yeah, just what I would expect from you, wanting to know who is gonna be in charge and who is gonna *look* like they're in charge. I mean, really, is that all you can think about? Do we even know what we're doing? What's our angle? What work needs to be done? And who is doing what? Are you so eager for the spotlight, for any spotlight, that you want to be the face for work you haven't even seen yet?" She looked at each person and landed on Jett. "Do we even have a hypothesis yet?"

Jett relaxed. A hypothesis. Proper work. She could do this. And it sounded like she would not be alone. Maybe Sam was the Brain...

"I have a couple of ideas," Andy chimed in.

Then again, maybe it was Andy. Maybe it was both. Could it be both? She would have to think about it, but not now. She was missing out on what they were saying and her notes would be incomplete. Jett tucked away her observations. She could sort it later.

And the work began.

Twenty minutes into the class, Andy had pages full of ideas, but no consensus. This was getting them nowhere. They hadn't even run the same range in data like Jett had in her research. She needed to tell them what she learned. She needed to help. Jett spoke up.

"Hey guys, data suggests love has many avenues we could explore. I mean, I looked it up. Want to talk about God or sex or family or romance? How about jungle love?" They all started laughing and Jett smiled. She was just getting warmed up.

"Did you know river otters love only one other river otter for life? Also, the mother is devoted to her babies. Did you know that narwhals mate in the spring, gestate their babies for over a year, and may not mate again for three years? How about the fact that cheetah males have sex with many female cheetahs, but female cheetahs also have many sexual partners? Is this still love? A dorcas gazelle only stays faithful to one partner if food is scarce, but the males go after many females if the climate and resources allow. Is that love or opportunity?"

Jett looked at Ruby, and continued. "What about a queen bee having, on average, seven partners, drones, and they each get seven to ten tries with her? Do you think that's a lot? Or maybe not. I don't know. But is that love? Owls tend to choose one love. Does that make it better? Is this the kind of love we're interested in finding out about and spending almost a year of our lives researching? What about the relevancy of romantic overtures to sexual satiation?"

"English please, professor," Carlos interrupted.

"I mean, does romance make sex more satisfying? Is there scientific evidence to support this? Does it even matter? Seriously, I'm not sure love even enters into that debate, so is it relevant? Do we really even know what love is? Should we maybe consider starting at the beginning, with common ground?" She had their attention; some were nodding and some were smiling. Even Ruby was paying attention. "I mean, what is love anyway, and how do *you* experience it?"

Carlos looked around and a flush rose in his skin. "Excuse me? Did you just ask about how I love?" He laughed nervously. "Um, I don't think I'm supposed to talk about it. I mean, I thought that was uncool."

Ruby purred. "Aw, come on Carlos, we all know you want to be seen as a Latin Lover. Why not tell us?"

Jett was floored. "What's a Latin Lover? Carlos, is that what you want to be? Are you Latin and a lover?"

Now everyone was nodding and laughing. Sam jumped in next. "Ruby, is it true that you prefer virtual dates to real ones? And do you play both ways? What's your stereotype? How do you love?"

Ruby clamped her mouth shut, raised her eyebrows, and started flexing her jaw. Jett watched a blush creep up Ruby's neck as she looked around her group. Ruby quickly shifted the collective attention to Andy. "Hey, Andy, your turn. Tell us about your love experience. Are you clear on all of this?"

Andy just shook his head and looked down at his notes.

"I'll tell you what I know," Sam volunteered. "What I know is that I don't know. I think Jett may be on to something, but I can't quite get at what she's trying to tell us. Jett, you got more to say?"

Jett nodded, back on solid ground. "Well, data suggests many things about love, and yet I find no consensus or concrete evidence that there is one definition or consistent experience among humans. Most of the animal kingdom has predictable trends among species, but not us."

She looked from Sam to Andy, expecting them to get what she was presenting. Watching their reactions, she continued. "I think we need to go back to the beginning and sort out a practical definition as well as categories for experiencing love. I mean, is love different for each person? What is the same? What makes it love?" Jett turned to the soccer star. "And Carlos? I'm serious. What is a Latin Lover?"

Again, her little group erupted in a fit of laughter.

"You are hysterical. I'm so … " Sam started. She shook her head and wiped at her eyes.

With a small smile, Andy looked down and blushed. Ruby was still laughing. Carlos put his arm around Jett, and she concentrated hard to keep herself from recoiling and to keep her shoulders from rising at the unexpected touch. Were their reactions indicative of love? Were they loving her? If so, what kind? What was she experiencing? Did she love them? Was what she felt normal? Loving? The same as the others?

She relaxed and decided that whether or not they loved her, they liked her. Maybe this was what people meant by friends. Maybe she was being accepted and appreciated for herself.

Ruby confirmed it. "Jett, I think you should be in charge, maybe even the face of this project. It'll require someone stepping up to defend our findings. I can help you with that, but I'm thinking you should do this."

And suddenly all eyes were on her in a way Jett had never experienced before. Should she accept this role? She had planned from the start on being the sole participant in the project. Should she step up and try this? Jett looked at her Core5, waiting for an answer. She thought about

The Breakfast Club. Did this make her the Brain? But it seemed they had other brains in this collective. Maybe she was the Entertainer. She made them laugh. She could be a Presenter. Isn't that what was meant by the face? That was a category *The Breakfast Club* forgot. Was it a category? She would have to consider that. Jett made a decision.

"All right. I'm in. I'll defend our work if you guys will help me put it all together. In the movie *The Breakfast Club,* they had an Athlete (she pointed to Carlos), a Princess (she pointed to Ruby), a Rebel, a Brain and a Basket Case. We don't have a Basket Case and I'm not sure who is our Brain or Rebel. Maybe we have two Brains. But I think they forgot the Face, the Spokesman. I'll do it and we can sort out the rest together. Yeah?"

The Core5 agreed. They had found their team, if not exactly their way to a hypothesis yet. Everyone smiled, even Ruby. And Jett was excited. She had a project, and now she also had friends.

Note to self: *Text Mother.*

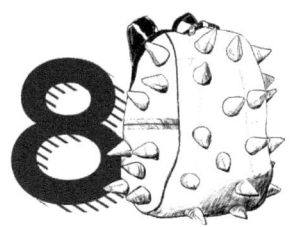

8

SEVERAL HOURS LATER, Jett removed the note from her phone and sent a text to her mother.

> FYI, my schedule just filled.
> Two important things happened today.
> I've been appointed lead on a pivotal project for my Foundations class.
> I also made friends; four of them.
> Thought you would want to know right away.

This was the most Jett had volunteered in weeks. She hoped her progress might erase the anxiety lining Mother's forehead.

A moment later she heard the response land on her phone.

> Jett! OMG, REALLY?!? BEST. NEWS. EVER! Thanks for sharing and I'll see you tonight. You can tell me all about it then :-).

    Jett nodded. It was a good day. It was a very good day.

    Suddenly she became aware of the stunning backdrop of her very privileged life. She heard the birds call. She watched the boats bob on the bay. She looked around at the other students milling about on the grassy field. There were so many, and they all seemed to be focused on one cluster. That's when she saw Ruby holding court. Jett strode over, excited by her new responsibilities and connections. She could hardly wait to get Ruby's input.

    Ruby was talking, "... yeah, I know right? I mean, like, did they really expect *me* to endorse that? For *my* following? You've got to be kidding! I've got a reputation, a brand, to protect. And that just wouldn't do!" Ruby sighed dramatically. "So not my thing. But nice try, Mediocres!" She used a hand to toss her hair over one shoulder.

    Jett watched Ruby take in her audience. She knew the minute she was spotted because Ruby's brows lifted—Jett had learned that usually was a sign of surprise—and drew together. What did that mean? Did Ruby need help with something? Could it be something she ate and now she had cramps? Was someone asking her embarrassing questions?

NEEDING NORMAL

Jett decided to jump into the conversation and save her new friend. "Hi, Ruby! I'm glad to see you. From our conversation earlier, I know you have more to say. Shall we continue?" She was so excited to have helped her friend out. Jett just knew this would erase the look on Ruby's face—and she was right. Ruby had a totally different look on her face now. Jett looked around at the crowd, expecting them also to be focused on Ruby, but they weren't. They were looking at her. She waited for Ruby's response, but none came.

Instead, a blonde cobra struck first. At least, that's how it felt. Suddenly the phrase "nest of vipers" came to mind, and Jett wanted to know if Ruby felt surrounded by danger.

"What are you doing here? Did you get lost or something? I've never seen you before. Maybe there's a school tour for the special needs kids or something? A charity? Do you even know where you are? Where's the rest of your group?" She turned to Ruby. "Did you invite one of your charities to tour the school today? Maybe *Love the Unlovables*?"

A red-headed viper sank her fangs in next. "Um, um, excuse me, um, Parasitic Amoeba, who gave you the right to interrupt Ruby? She was just telling us about a sponsorship deal she turned down. OhmiGAWD! Did that loser company send *you* to ask her to reconsider? Who gave you the right to even speak to Ruby, and like that? Like you had a relationship? Do you honestly think she even knows your name?"

This one Jett could answer. "Yes. Ruby knows my name. I am Jett Harper." As for the other queries—where to begin?

But there was no time. A tall and willowy boy struck next. "Yeah, Boo. Whatevs. I'd say 'you do you,' but I'm not sure you should. I mean, really? What's with wearing your big brother's shirts and carrying a kid's backpack? Is it a hand-me-down? Did you steal it or just not have enough money for a real bag?" He turned so she could see his Givenchy backpack, a twin to the one her uncle carried on weekends. "Are you here for a makeover? I mean, if so, this is some serious work and we might need to start like, oh, last year? Also, some stalking skills to track Ruby down at her new school." He turned to Ruby. "Want me to call security?"

Ruby gave a small shake of her head and kept her arms folded, watching them sink their fangs into Jett. She didn't lash out herself, but she also didn't stop them as the venom continued to flow.

Jett went from helpful to baffled to mad. Really mad. Who were these people? First, she lashed back at the male model. "Um, hi. Yeah, you." She didn't even think about it. She looked him straight in the face. "Spiketus Rex is a very cool pack, and I'm proud to carry it instead of an old man's backpack. My uncle carries the same one you do on his time off from the office." Now she turned to the blonde who started it all. "I'm not lost. Ruby is in my group and you are not, so could you maybe not interrupt before she has a chance to respond? I wasn't speaking to you." She looked expectantly at Ruby, who simply sat there, frozen. She definitely needed Jett's help. Was she under a spell or something? Jett was really worried. What had happened to her new friend? Maybe she should go get backup, but she couldn't leave Ruby in that viper's nest.

"Just ignore them, Ruby. Talk to me about love. I know you know. You had so much to say earlier. Please, just ignore them and tell me about it. I've got an excellent memory. I will actively listen and take down the notes later. Focus on me, Ruby. Tell me about love."

Ruby remained impassive. Jett watched the crowd's curiosity pique as the silence stretched.

Jett had been studying body language in order to fulfill Mother's assignment that she make friends with the "right" teens and learn how to lead. Some body postures said the group was entertained, others were indicating discomfort. Ruby's body language just read—well, blank. Jett made a mental note to spend more time learning about postures and facial expressions. She sighed. How was she going to get them both out of this one? She looked around for the rest of her group, but Sam and Andy weren't there, and not even Carlos. Dang. Carlos would know what to do with Ruby. Sam probably would have, too.

Straightening her spine, Jett spoke directly to Ruby. "Ruby, it's okay. We can talk some more about love later, but for now, I just need you to step away from these ridiculously rude people. Come with me. I can help you."

At that, Ruby turned her head, taking in her loyal audience. Jett thrilled at the progress. Ruby had turned her head! She looked around, too. The crowd had tightened their circle and Ruby was caught in the middle. Extraction would be difficult.

"Okay, Ruby, now take a step forward. We can get through this. We can … " Jett reached out her hand.

Finally, Ruby spoke. "Um, Jett? You shouldn't be here. Seriously, this isn't okay." She crossed her arms over her chest. "Just go. Seriously. I don't want to see this happen again."

Jett frowned. Was Ruby telling her to go without her? Was Ruby trying to save her while she was trying to save Ruby? How was this going to work? She saw the blonde, the redhead, and the model vipers form a tight line next to Ruby, mimicking Ruby's posture with their arms folded. Was she just supposed to leave her here? What else could she do?

Jett hefted her pack up onto her shoulder and grabbed the straps. Maybe she could swing it around like a bat at a baseball game and knock them all over like bowling pins. If only the spikes were real. She could defeat the enemy and save Ruby. But Ruby had other plans.

"Go, Jett. Go now."

Jett felt Ruby watching her as she hesitated. She watched Ruby for signs she was ready to run, but she wasn't. She was trapped in the circle, and yet she had commanded Jett to go. Ruby was caught but Jett wasn't and so she listened.

She turned and left, hearing laughter follow her. It sounded to her like snakes swallowing their prey. Jett shuddered. This was horrible. Ruby had saved her but had fallen victim in the process. It wasn't until she heard Ruby's laugh that Jett felt defeated. Great. Just great. It occurred to her that her first impression of Ruby as the reigning princess may have been right. Maybe Ruby wasn't in danger at all, but instead was their leader. What did that mean for Jett? How would their friendship work? A notification from her phone distracted her and she tripped on a root. She fell. Hard. She heard even more laughter. Jett looked up to see the crowd watching her. No one came after her. Still lying face down on the ground, she reached for her phone to check the missed text. It was from Ruby.

> Sorry, Jett.

Did the message mean they were friends again? Was she supposed to try to save her, again? Jett didn't want to get back up. Turning her head to look back at the group, she saw that boy talking about something. It seemed to require his whole body. As he spoke, his over-the-top movements kept the crowd entertained. He was riveting, captivating. But Ruby wasn't looking at him. She was watching Jett lie there on the ground.

Jett felt the first tear fall as she gingerly lowered her face back into the dirt.

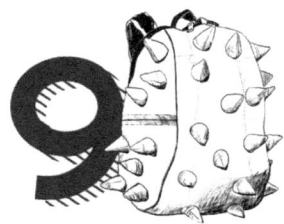

A TALL MAN with a regal presence stood by the window looking out to the bay. When he heard footsteps stop at the open door to his office, he turned slowly, graceful hands clasped loosely behind his back. Jett watched him take in her presence. He reminded her of how she thought a Moorish emir would look. She felt his eyes on her, taking her measure, and she took a step back. This was not what she had signed up for. This counselor was acting like a real counselor, like the therapists in Mother's circle, the ones who spent their days in... heavy sigh. Yeah. Did he know Mother? OMG. How was this going to work? He was supposed to be just an academic "counselor," not a therapist type of counselor. Right?

Jett looked around more carefully. Yeah, mmm-hmm, he certainly looked like one of those; like one of the ones who spent their days in offices like Mother's. And this place? This sure looked like a therapist's office. She pulled her Spiketus Rex up on her shoulder, her armor closer to her body.

"I like your backpack, Jett." He waited a beat, but continued when she didn't respond. "You are Jett, right? Is your pack some sort of mutant turtle shell thing? I can't really tell from here. Want to come in? Tell me about it?"

Jett shook her head no. She most certainly did *not* want to come in. She stood frozen in the doorway and she knew he saw this. He seemed to see everything. Definitely trained as a therapist/counselor. He studied her rigid posture, her screaming silence. The man turned back towards the window and tried again. "I've been looking forward to meeting you. Please come in. Make yourself comfortable." He spoke loud enough to invite her, not quite a command but not something she could ignore. Jett didn't want to, but she took one more step.

He kept his back to her as she fought her instinct to flee, rambling in a friendly way. "I was just watching the world outside. So much to see, so much to sort through, so much to choose. What do you see, Jett?"

Jett looked around. Was this some sort of trick? White stucco walls lined with bookshelves housed an interesting mix of novels and non-fiction as well as framed black-and-white photos. It looked a lot like the other offices in the administration wing, but with one curious difference. The books were not chosen and arranged for their visual appeal. These were a visual riot. These well-worn books were for learning. This fascinated her, drawing her in while simultaneously triggering her reflex to run. Knowledge was important here. Lives changed here. She took it all in, including the man quietly watching the world and waiting. She decided to get this over with.

"Good afternoon, Mr. Williams. I *am* Jett Harper and you probably already know why I am here. Shall we just wrap this up? Do you need more from me than the original work to give me a signature?"

"Ah! Jett Harper speaks eloquently! Good afternoon to you, Ms. Harper." He turned to face her. "Yes, I'd like to see what you brought me. Want to tell me how you managed to fail your first paper here at Presidio Prep? The administration tends to admit overachievers. Your file presents you not only as an overachiever but maybe *the* overachiever of your class." He reached out his hand in a silent demand for the offending paper.

Jett let her pack fall to the floor as she handed over her work. The tall man with all-seeing eyes accepted it. He looked down at it, and then back up at Jett.

"Mind if I read this?"

Jett shook her head, but he was already reading it.

"No, sir. I am guessing that is part of your process before I can get your signature, and why we need fifteen minutes. I think Ms. Diaz graded unfairly. She might actually be impaired. Maybe you can see why?"

The counselor looked up, surprised by her summation. "Do you, now? Mind telling me what she asked for and why you think she graded this unfairly?"

"I'll tell you exactly why I think that. Ms. Diaz asked for a personal essay on love. I delivered an essay I personally wrote on the requested topic, including a strong hypothesis, supporting data, and footnotes. She failed me! I expect it is because of my unusual insight for my age and my ability to add things together. I believe she might think I plagiarized, but I assure you, I did not! This is my personal work. I have never had to copy others. When I challenged her grading system, she offered me a secondary assignment due today and said that I must get a signature from either my parents or you. I chose your signature, and I have written a rant which may or may not satisfy her new requirements." Jett folded her arms and tried to stop rocking on her heels, but the rocking felt too comforting, too necessary. She was barely holding it all in. What if he took offense to what she had just shared? She started rocking more instead of less. Was he trying to hide a smile? What could that mean?

Mr. Williams watched her carefully. "What did she ask for this time?"

It sounded like he was honestly curious.

"This time Ms. Diaz asked that I write about how I experience love, which, I might point out, is not the same thing." Jett shook her head. "I know she is the teacher and I'm sure her credentials are just as well vetted as the students, but really! Is this even an appropriate topic for my age?"

He held up a hand and cut her off. "Actually Jett, all of our staff are more carefully vetted and selected than the student body. There is a waiting list to be a part of the teaching team here and it's longer than the waiting list to become a student here." He paused to let that sink in. "Do you know why?"

She shook her head. It certainly didn't seem that way from her experience. Maybe he was misinformed. If he was correct, if the staff *was* an elite group of educators, why would they choose this school? Was it an experiment of some kind? An experiment on human youth? Were they trying to prove something? Maybe they were here to test an outlier hypothesis about leadership and overachievers. He did mention overachievers earlier. Jett squinted and studied him carefully.

The Counselor set down her paper and folded his hands behind his back, returning his gaze out the window.

"It's because of students like you, Jett. The list of over-qualified applicants who want to work with students as smart as you could line the walls of this entire building."

"But I don't understand," she said. She knew her parents considered Presidio Prep to be prestigious, maybe even unique or revolutionary. But hearing it from a knowledgeable source surprised her.

"I know you don't, Jett," he said, turning back around. "And I'm here because of that. I'm here to bridge the gap between your understanding of Ms. Diaz and her understanding of you. Shall I go on, or did you have more to add?"

She knew he was staring at her, but didn't meet his eyes. Her rocking slowed. She turned her attention to the photos on the shelves. He waited.

When she broke the silence, Jett shared her hypothesis on group projects. She told him that most of the work in a group project was done by one, maybe two individuals, yet the grade was evenly distributed. She explained that this was unfair, like paying someone to work when they didn't. She told him she was tired of being the one to do all the work.

"Did you know that many of my peers are unsure about how they experience love? I know. I asked them. Today. They don't know, either. And I also know none of them failed their initial assignment. How is this right for her to ask us? And why am I the only one being asked to write on how I experience it?" Jett started frantically pacing, eyes darting from image to image. Was she really the only one struggling here?

Mr. Williams moved from near the window to behind his desk. Both hands firmly planted on stacks of paper, he leaned forward. "Jett," he said. "Jett, remember to breathe. I have answers. Can I share them?" He waited for her pacing to slow.

"Jett. You are right."

She looked up at this.

"Yes, Jett. You are right. This practice seems totally unfair to you. And you did it anyway. Well done. If I understand you correctly, you want me to sign off on a personally written research paper on love, and then talk with your teacher about her unfair practices. Does that about sum it up?"

She met his eyes and nodded.

He nodded back slowly and signed the top sheet of her paper. "Okay, then. Anything else?"

She hesitated, then decided to see what else he knew. "Mr. ... I'm sorry I forgot to confirm your name. You *are* Mr. Williams, right?" He inclined his head at her.

"Okay." Jett conceded. She stopped fiddling with the straps on her pack. "Good. Mr. Williams, my mother asked me to watch and learn from the kids who are succeeding. And to also figure out who to be friends with. But I don't understand. I don't know who to be friends with because I don't know what constitutes a friend. I don't think I've ever had one. How do you find those? Is it like a scavenger hunt? And who is succeeding at all things? How do I know who they are? What am I supposed to do when I figure that out? *Wait!* Is that who I am supposed to be friends with? What does that even ... " Jett's eyes were getting larger, her speech more frantic. This was inconceivable.

"Whoa, whoa, *whoa there*, Jett! Slow your roll. Let's talk about this. You've just given me a lot of information to consider and some assignments that I take very seriously. I want to get it right and give you what you need. Will

NEEDING NORMAL

you come see me again?" He sighed in relief as she slowly nodded. Returning the gesture, he started rearranging his desk, keeping everything in order. He looked down at his papers before meeting her gaze with one of his own. "Jett, thank you for being here. Our school needs you, and I'm going to speak with that teacher. I'm going to consider your mother's assignments and how to approach them, too. Don't you worry."

She reached for her pack and heaved it into place as she approached the door. Speaking over her shoulder, she added, "Your picture with the giraffes is from Safari West. Did you know they have a new baby? Did you know giraffes are the world's tallest mammal? At birth, calves stand up to six and a half feet high. That makes him already taller than you." Jett thought she caught a look of surprise on his face, but couldn't be sure. Maybe he thought that baby giraffes were small? Ah well, it didn't matter. She had a signature and a paper to turn in.

As she entered her Foundations classroom, Jett smiled to herself. Ms. Diaz was there putting her supplies back into her bag.

"Well, hello there, Jett Harper! I am guessing you came to bring me a signature and a new paper?"

"Yes, Ms. Diaz. I did. I do. I have a signature and a new paper for you." She handed them over.

"You look happy, Jett. I like this look on you. I am hoping I had some part in this smile. Is that true?"

"Oh, yes! You are the reason I am smiling. Ms. Diaz, I hope your day is..." Jett tilted her head, thinking of the right word. "Enlightening."

She was still smiling as she left, daydreaming about the talking to Ms. Diaz would be receiving from Counselor Williams. The warm sun matched her mood. Today was turning out better than she expected.

10

DAYS LATER, ON a walk across campus, Jett noted leaves turning. The riot of colors didn't compare to the photos she had seen from an autumn in New England, but it still announced the seasons, and she was happy with the subtle shift. Her team was pulling together on the project, in a manner of speaking. They were still sorting out what to say, let alone how to test it, but still it felt like progress. And they had time.

At home, she had re-watched *The Breakfast Club*, trying to sort out if there could be more than one Brain in the group. What about the Basket Case? Who was that? The character was so obvious in the movie. Was it possible to be a Basket Case and be covertly broken, covertly challenged? Could there be one and she just didn't recognize it? If so, whom? She needed to understand her peers.

She had added *The Perks of Being a Wallflower* to her movie studies. There were definitely nuggets of wisdom in there to analyze—the power of connection, the poignancy of influence.

With so much to think about, so much tickling her brain, Jett wandered towards an as-yet unexplored building on campus. She heard music painting window sills and escaping under doors. So many sounds, so many emotions pouring through. Jett felt compelled to follow the pull. She tried to enter several doors. All were locked. With her hand on yet another doorknob, she looked at the windows and thought about how to get inside, where she needed to be. And, surprisingly, the knob turned. No creaks to this door. Silently she stepped into the building, without interrupting all she heard, all she felt.

Doors lined the hallways, portals into hope, heartbreak, wonder, and worry. Jett felt understood. Jett felt like she belonged. She knew these things. She lived them. Her fingers fluttered and tapped. Her body started to dance as she was called deeper into the building, passing the doors leading to the not-quite-right songs. She needed more. She sought out the soul-searing song of pain.

Light, from windows high above, converged to spotlight a lone and unexpected figure, someone singing. Jett heard it, felt it. She sought it out, and froze in place as the door shut silently behind her. Not what she expected. It was her friend Sam, from the Core5 project.

Jett watched her stand in the middle of a grand but bare stage, pouring out her heart. The auditorium was a cavernous space, empty of people but full of emotions. She stared at her, but Sam didn't see anything external. Eyes closed, muscles coiled, Sam looked ready to spring, even as music poured forth, crowding the empty space. Courage, craving, rage and regret. Everything seared straight into Jett's soul. Under the weight, she sunk to the ground. Her backpack thudded but she didn't hear it.

How? How did a few tones strung together have the power to level physical objects? How could it hold her captive and expose her tender heart? Unable to voluntarily move, Jett felt drugged. Her chin hit her chest and a deep shuddering breath racked her frame. So much to process, but she understood. This. This was a part of Love. The shadow part? Yes, but still a part of it.

As the last notes escaped, Sam opened her eyes and looked around, gathering her bearings. She saw Jett and stiffened, then growled. "What. The. Actual. Hell!" Sam stalked closer. She towered over Jett. "Who let you in? How did you get here? Who knows? What did you hear? How dare you…"

Jett felt the tears running down her face. They warmed her, even as she noted goosebumps rising on her skin. Her entire body shook. A low visceral keening left Jett's heart open for Sam to see.

Sam's approach shifted. She softened visibly under Jett's transfixed gaze. She heard Sam start to wail with her, even as she felt Sam slowly crouch by her side. Jett was rigid with nervous system overload but also curious as to the way Sam's song wrapped around her own. She was both in and out of her body, mind silently observing and audibly processing, at the same time.

Sam sang for all she was worth. She let the notes take her down the path towards Jett. Sam gave voice to the unvoiceable and wove it around Jett's pain. Her notes held them both. Sam's voice carried them back into the moment and gently deposited them both onto the floor.

"Hey, Jett. Where did you go?"

"Where did you take me? Sam, how did you do that? Was that some kind of magic? What just happened?"

Sam sighed. "OhmiGAWD, Jett. I didn't know you were there. I thought I was alone. I thought I could just, you know, let it all out, some things going on. I thought I might be able to practice a few riffs in here because the acoustics are amazing; but then I started thinking and then just feeling, and getting found in the music..." She looked at Jett. "How long were you here? What did you hear?"

"I heard love. I heard hard, haunting moments and lasting, longing, love. I heard my heartbeat. I heard the sun shine. I heard it all." Jett wilted, no longer shaking, no longer in autonomic overwhelm, but heavy with revelations. She felt weary.

The two girls sat in silence for a moment. Then Sam spoke. "You know you can't tell anyone, right? I mean, you did break into a building that requires permissions and I'm guessing you didn't get any. You just came. That makes you pretty badass, but you heard things not really meant for you."

Jett shook her head. "No, Sam. I didn't hear things. I felt things. I felt seen. Understood. Free. I felt..." She tilted her head and considered how to explain her experience. "I felt completely free to be me."

Sam sighed. "I didn't think getting into trouble would be your thing. And free to be you? I don't see you shying away from that in what I've seen. You *are* you, Jett. You're just not in Kansas anymore, Dorothy."

And once again, a classmate was confusing names or characters. Did Sam not know who she was? But she did just say "Jett." She had to think about this. Jett knew she was missing something, but not what nor how to sort it out. Names and misnaming, mistaken identities.... wait! Could Sam be referring to Dorothy from *The Wizard of Oz* by L. Frank Baum? That would tie together Dorothy and Kansas. But how did it apply to her? Jett sighed heavily. She had so much to think about.

"You need to go," Sam said, standing up. "You know, we aren't *all* friends outside of class, right? We can't just hang out and you can't sneak up on people."

Jett slowly lifted her dropped backpack, processing the lessons Sam was trying to teach her. She needed to go. Check. You can't sneak up on people. Check. We aren't friends outside of class. Che— Wait. What? Friendships had timer switches like some lights and appliances in a smart home? Huh. She didn't know that. She wanted to understand, to know more.

"Okay, Sam. But I need to know a few things." She looked Sam straight in the eyes, trying to convey how very important this was to her.

Sam's eyebrows drew down and her lips pursed in a closed "o". Squinting, she turned to fully face Jett. "Yeah? What?"

"Well, a few things really; but first let's talk about what's relevant to our project. Your song was so much. Was it about love?"

Startled, Sam peered closely at Jett and slowly nodded. "Yeah. It was for me. But it's private, okay?"

Jett nodded solemnly. She understood private. She understood not being able to tell the world, or even people she was speaking with, about everything she thought. She knew all about having to choose not only what to share, but how to share it. This was the most exhausting part of her life and, unfortunately, also the most consistent. Jett could keep Sam's secrets.

"Next?" asked Sam.

"You said we aren't all friends outside of class and that I know this. But I don't. I don't know this, Sam. How does this work? Is that why Ruby was socially inept in the quad the other day, when she was surrounded by her court? Is there a book I missed on the timing of friends and how to determine when and where the label applies? I don't understand, but I'm trying to. Will you explain it to me so I can get it right and be like ... be like—normal?"

Jett stood motionless, waiting for Sam's reaction to her most painful secret. She felt awkward and ashamed. And for her, the moment lasted too long. But Sam appeared not to have even noticed. Was that how most people were, failing to see other's painful truths? Relaxing a little, Jett hoped so. It certainly would make her life a lot less stressful.

Instead, Sam was flabbergasted. "Dude! How'd you get so screwed up on how things work?"

"I ... " Jett thought for a moment. "Movies."

Sam nodded like that made sense to her. "Okay, so here's the thing. I can't believe I'm admitting this, but movies can teach us a lot. Some true, some not. Watch *The Hate U Give*. It oughtta help you get more 'bout life in the real world."

"Wait. Aren't we in the real world?" asked Jett, arms akimbo.

"No, Dorothy. This ain't Kansas." Sam started humming the prelude to *Somewhere Over the Rainbow*.

Jett nodded. That was obvious. Her mind tuned back in when Sam's humming turned into soft singing. She strained to listen. As she left, Jett caught a few words of the song: *"Why, oh, why can't I?"*

She had gone looking for a place to ponder and had stumbled into a place to *feel*. Feeling unfiltered and processing complex problems was too much. They exhausted her even as the last notes filled her with longing and hope. For now, all she wanted was to go home, crawl into bed and take a nap. Love and life would have to wait.

11

TO JETT, TODAY was the toughest day. Ever. And, she was glad to be home, to be alone in her space, a place uncensored where she could try to figure out the why. Trying to sort out the underlying reason, Jett felt uneasy. She bounced on the balls of her feet, pinched at her neck and twirled her wrists, but to no avail. Nothing worked. Unable to pinpoint a specific event, a specific trigger, she recognized a fact: it was just *tough*. Undefined unease exhausted her. Jett assumed this feeling of overwhelm was how others would react, and more research confirmed her suspicions. This was normal. So why did she still feel uneasy? Would it follow her throughout the weekend? Jett looked out her window and watched autumn leaves fly away. She'd like to fly away from unanchored anxiety. Looking for comfort, she donned her favorite hoodie.

Depression and anxiety were the bane of her generation and Jett was glad to know she wasn't alone. She *probably* wasn't overreacting. If only she could pinpoint the reason for all her angst, then she wasn't diagnosable. This would be more evidence she was normal. But what *exactly* had set off the constriction in her throat, the burning in her eyes? She looked up from her computer and blinked rapidly. Her mind wouldn't stop spinning. She needed a break. Her parents were still at work and she was on her own. Jett stood up, stretched and looked out the window. She bit her lip.

The pup with no name was outside. He seemed to sense her. Their eyes locked and she ran out the front door to go see him.

Ben looked up as the door shut to see an unsmiling and resolute Jett approaching him. She needed puppy time and she needed answers. Jett hesitated on the top step, then saw that Ben was bringing the puppy to her. Maybe he knew the answers? At least she could talk with him without a filter. He was closer to a peer than her parents and yet, like her parents, he knew how to listen actively. Maybe all she needed was a sounding board. It was worth a try. He had been helpful in the past. And he wasn't vested in the outcome, in her success, so she could rely on him not to overreact.

"Hi, chum. Why so glum?" The pup was jumping and shaking with excitement, but settled as he looked up at Ben. He waited for Jett to approach, tail still thumping.

"Ben, something is wrong, but I don't know what." She reached out for the pup, letting her outstretched hands dangle in the crisp air. Purposefully not making eye contact, Jett waited for them to approach. She crouched down.

"Oh, really?" asked Ben. "Just one thing?"

Shocked, Jett looked up at him. *Was there usually more than one thing wrong?* What a disturbing revelation. The pup looked up at Ben, who nodded to him before he approached Jett. They connected and her body visibly relaxed. She liked touching the puppy's fur. It helped her mind stop spinning, even now, knowing more than one thing could be wrong.

"I don't know what to say, Jett. Tell me about your day."

"I don't know, Ben. My day seems irrelevant." She waited for a new question.

Ben cleared his throat. "Jett, look at me. I've been there." He waited for eye contact. "Your days are not irrelevant. Fill me in. Go back as far as you need to."

Jett stared into Ben's eyes, gauging his sincerity. She tried to assess his ability to really get her life.

"I am a high school freshman. My days *are* irrelevant. Until I started high school and actually failed at something for the first time, I thought my life was not only relevant but crucial. Now I know better. I am a member of society, yet not even legally recognized, and my voice is nil. It isn't small. It is nil.

"So far, I have learned that, just like in the movie *The Breakfast Club*, in my world there are Athletes and Princesses, Rule Breakers and Rule Makers, Brokens and Brains. I have learned there is much I don't know and shockingly, even more I don't want to know. I don't understand how friends work. I mean, social protocols alone, the nuances are astounding. Did you know there are time periods for friendships? For example, I can be friends with someone in class but not outside, or sometimes, friends are friends in both. How do I know which is which? I have learned the categories, but not how to classify. And I know *nothing* about love, which is my biggest problem. I mean, we just had midterms. All good, except my project on love for the Foundations class. And now, winter semester is fast approaching and my entire GPA is in jeopardy. I don't know what to do about the big project.

"What I do know is that music can break you and remake you. I know this pup with no name is the bright spot in my life, and yet I don't know how he receives love. Does he even feel it? Or return it? How *exactly* do puppies feel love? Do they express it? How do we know? Are humans and puppies the same?"

She paused, expecting an answer, but Ben just stared at her. She watched him swallow. She watched him slowly open his mouth and then close it. Again. Open. Close. Open. Close. It was a silent staring contest. Finally, he swallowed again and began to speak.

"You ask the most curious questions. Do you know that? As for the answers? Where to start." He sighed.

"Okay. Love. That's the main thing, right? The one you're really puzzled by. We talked about it before and it's still coming up so let's just start there, with the most pressing issue."

"You know you're rambling, right?" She wondered if this was a sign of his enthusiasm or a signal of his angst. Was talking about love somehow causing him stress? Maybe he didn't know about it, either.

"Oh. Yeah. Right!" He paused to regroup. "Um, okay. Let's talk about one theory of love. Ready?" As she nodded, he seemed to settle into his message. "I looked it up after our last conversation. I wanted to sort out a better explanation, and there's this whole thing called the five love languages. Do you know about that?"

Ben looked up at Jett before fiddling with the pups ears again. Occasionally he signaled for pup to sit or stand or circle. Rewarding pup intermittently seemed to keep him focused and Jett filed all of this away for later reproduction. "Um, Jett?"

Jett shook her head, surprised. Did he know she was answering him? "I thought there were more than five languages." Maybe Ben meant the most commonly used. But what did that have to do with love? And, if there was something called a "love language," could she learn it, just like French or Latin?

"Well, it kind of goes like this. People give and receive love naturally. It's part of how we express ourselves, and yet not everyone does that the same way. It's like we speak in different accents, different languages. So, this dude named

Dr. Chapman came up with a list of five ways that covers both how we give and receive love." He looked at Jett and the pup again. Both were listening attentively. "You sure you haven't uncovered this in your research?"

"Nope, not yet. But I'm gonna take notes. What's his name again?" Jett pulled out her phone and opened it to her favorite note-taking app. This was certainly not what she had expected.

"Dr. Chapman. Gary Chapman. Anyway, he figured out this thing and it seems pretty accurate to me."

And so it went. The sun set on Jett playing tug-of-war with the puppy and Ben telling her all he could think of about love.

Jett stood on her tiptoes and rolled back to her heels, several times in quick succession. She was excited, so she interrupted. "Wow, Ben. I think my love language may be 'words of affirmation.'" Her entire face lit up as she found relevance for her own life. He may be onto something, she thought.

"You do, do you? Well Jett, to be honest, I think all of us are all the things. I also think there are just some we respond to more naturally than others. I'm not sure we give and receive love the same ways, but it makes sense that we probably do. Do you praise people you love?" Now Ben was genuinely curious.

"I don't love anyone," she admitted freely, even as she smiled at the pup and continued with their game of tug.

NEEDING NORMAL 93

"What?" Ben took a step back. Unthinking, he reached for the pup while processing this unexpected development. The pup dutifully returned to his side for connection.

Jett didn't understand the pup with no name's reaction. She had been busy playing with him, but now he stood next to Ben, who was rhythmically soothing them both. She was puzzled.

"I don't think I love anyone," she amended, defensively. "I may be wrong. I still haven't figured out what specifically love is, for sure. It's good to know how to experience it, but I'd like to know what it is, too. What is love?"

Ben bit his top lip and frowned. "You...you..." A huff escaped him. He squinted and lowered his voice, talking to himself, as he tried to figure out how to answer. "Love is... *deep breath*," She heard him counting: *"1-2-3-4 and breathe, dammit, 1-2-3-4 breathe."*

She waited patiently, watching Ben carefully. The pup hadn't left his side, even to fetch his favorite tug toy. She tilted her head to consider. Ben was using breathing regulation techniques that she learned from Mother when she was wearing her therapist hat. Did Ben go to therapy? Is that where he learned to breathe and count? Did he know most people did it silently? She watched him open his eyes and continue the rhythmic breathing without audible prompting. *Well done*, she thought, feeling a surge of pride towards him.

Ben looked off into the distance.

"You know that feeling you get when something really warms your heart? When it beats faster, but in a good way? When warmth envelops you and you feel valued? I think that's love. Do you know what I'm talking about? When Pup looks up at you and you can't help but smile? Love. When he snuggles into you or wags his tail in anticipation of your play or when your parents want to know how school went. When they drive you each morning. When your friends are your friends everywhere, not just in selective places. When you give up the pup to better someone else's life." Ben stopped speaking and let his examples hang in the air between them. His eyes watered.

Pup sat at attention. No longer playing, he watched the entire conversation as if it were a tennis match, head swiveling from speaker to speaker.

Jett checked Ben's autonomic responses. He was breathing deeply but seemed ready to collapse. He was holding his body rigidly. She was sure that must be taking monumental effort. Ben needed to relax. She wondered if she should approach him, stand closer, play him a song to match his visible pain or whether Pup should do something besides watch and wait.

Fascinated by everything he had just told her, Jett felt she was on the verge of understanding this thing called love, but now Ben stopped? She wanted to encourage him; he was onto something. Deciding not to approach, or play music, she found no valid response but to ask. Maybe it

NEEDING NORMAL

would help if he knew his impact and that she was actively listening, too. "What's wrong, Ben? Your list gives me a lot to consider. Did you not have more to add or was something inaccurate? Why are you sad? You sound like you might cry. Are you needing to cry? I can play you a sad song if that will help." She fiddled with her phone, trying to find it quickly.

"No, Jett. None of that," he said, offering her a wavering smile. "It's Pup. He's amazing. Just look at him."

She looked. They both did. The pup with no name met their joint gaze with tail wags, pants, and eye contact ping-ponging between them. She wondered what was wrong. Pup looked healthy and happy to her.

"Pretty soon he's going to go off to school. I didn't expect to get so attached, that it would be so hard to let him go," Ben admitted.

She tried to process this. "I don't understand. School is the goal, right? It's a good thing. What's so bad about Pup going to school?"

"I will tell you more, but first? I think you are right. I think it's time to name Pup and I think you should do it."

"I—what? Okay, but what?" She put her phone down and focused back on the pup, who was still busy eavesdropping on their conversation. He caught her eye and started wagging his tail, but slowly this time.

"What are we going to call him?" Ben asked her softly.

Her answer was swift. "I have two thoughts. Kenobi, because, you know—Ben," she said, pointing to Ben, "Kenobi," pointing to the pup. "They just go together."

A tear slid down Ben's cheek as he shook his head. More tears. He cleared his throat. "And the other choice? Your other thought for a name?"

She thought about that one tear. Did he not get her reference? Ben Kenobi? *Star Wars*? The Jedi Master? And if not, would he understand her second name choice? She might have to explain.

"My other name choice would be Yoda. Because he is wise and entertaining, even when I don't speak his language."

Jett watched him carefully for comprehension. Ben seemed to get it. He seemed to like this better. He even laughed a little.

"Yoda it is then," he said.

Jett wasn't sure what to do now. Was it appropriate to ask more about love? But that had made him cry, and he had already told her so much. Was it okay to ignore him now and play with Yoda? Ben seemed to need some playtime with the pup now too, maybe more than she did. Picking up the tug toy and handing it to him, she decided it was time to go back inside and get to work.

"Ben, thank you for telling me about love and the languages. Thank you for letting me play with the pup. I mean Yoda. I need to get back to work now, and I think you need to play with Yoda. Will you be all right?"

Ben looked up at the question and saw the lights of a car approaching. "I'll be fine, Jett. Besides, I think your parents are home. I bet they'll be wanting family time now, too. See you soon?"

Jett nodded and lifted a hand in farewell. The toughest day had turned into a tender evening. "Bye, Ben. See you soon."

12

TUCKED INTO A popular corner of the school's cafe, four of the Core5 waited. Today, they were meeting outside of class to see if they could pin down this project. It had to be done. Andy was last to arrive. And he was not alone. Jett frowned. Having never seen Andy outside of their mutual classes, she hadn't thought of him as having a social circle, of having friends. She heard them laughing and wondered why. She looked more carefully, trying to find the source of such joy. And she noted his circle of friends all had the beautiful caramel and mocha coloring of the latte coffees being served around the cafe. Not one was the color of steamed milk, like her. Did that mean she wouldn't qualify to call him friend outside of the classroom?

Jett peeked at his "signature piece," his socks. Sure enough, he was wearing wildly patterned footwear, the likes of which she had never seen on anybody but him. Who was Andy in this circle of friends? What role did he play? She watched him wave to his friends as they retreated to a spot on the other side of the room.

Testing her newly formed *Breakfast Club* sorting system everywhere, Ruby and Carlos were easy to classify: Carlos was the Athlete and Ruby was the Princess. But, Andy and Sam were harder for her to pinpoint. She considered they might both be Brains. But the pain she overheard pouring from Sam's music the other day might make her better suited to the Broken/Basket Case category. That just left the Rebel role open for Jett to assume. But how did that work? Wasn't that a better fit for Sam? Jett recognized she didn't have enough information to finish casting the roles. She looked up from her internal analysis. *Time to wade into the conversation,* she thought, as she mentally rejoined the group.

Sam was playing the interrogator. "Seriously, Carlos, does everything relate back to soccer? Is that how you see love? Like a game? Winners and losers? Hearts passed from player to player, like a ball traveling the field? Teams and trials? Compromise and contracts?"

Carlos was smiling and nodding. Jett watched Carlos look around as his nods slowed. No one else was smiling. Sam looked like she was calculating advanced math in her head. Andy's face registered surprise, and Ruby's face pinched in concern before she smoothed it into one of indifference.

"Players. They perfect the game, don't they?" Ruby said dismissively. "What if they actually miss the goal? What if they don't score?"

"Hey, hey, Linda! *No!* That's not what I... I mean. Kinda but I didn't..." Brows drawn down and face looking unusually serious, Carlos shrugged and trailed off.

Andy sighed, Sam smirked, and Jett watched. What was happening? Carlos reached for Ruby's hand and started quietly pleading. She pulled away, looking upset. Jett swallowed; their quiet conversation looked painful. She wanted to—but knew she shouldn't—watch anymore. She turned her entire body away to give them some privacy.

Sam lasered in on Andy. "What about you? Do you have an idea we can use for our project? You've been awfully quiet. What do you have to contribute?"

Andy shrugged his shoulders and shook his head. His hair flopped over his glasses.

Jett focused on his facial expression, trying to read it.

"I mean, of course I know *something* about love," Andy said defensively. "I *do* have a family, an Indian family, so *of course* we are close. We love each other. When I get home from school each day, my Dada asks about my day and what work I have left to complete. My Dadi is usually in the kitchen putting together a snack for me."

Ruby started snickering. When she looked around and realized she was the only one, she defended herself by repeating the names. "A Dada and a Dadi? What are you, four?"

Andy shook his head in disgust and continued. "Dadi and Dada are my maternal grandparents, Ruby. They deserve respect."

Ruby's mouth hung open in the shape of an "O" before she shut it. She had the grace to look down and say nothing more.

Andy looked around. At Sam's nod, he continued. "My sister is younger than me and could be anywhere in our home, but I hear her. She's lively and loud. For example, as soon as she knows Dadi has made me something to eat, she shows up to steal my food, or try to get Dadi to make something special for her as well. By the time my parents come home, all the schoolwork must be done. Chores are finished. We are scrubbed clean and ready for family time. But that is pretty stereotypical for first-generation immigrant culture, isn't it? I don't know any differently, but is that so different from the rest of you?"

The group nodded at him. "Well, that's all I know about love. I don't see how that can be any more than the paper I've already written, that we've all already written. I assumed we all kind of turned in the same thing. But I guess that doesn't matter. What does matter is that we're all good. Since we all passed, it's clear this will be a straightforward assignment."

Jett sank lower in her seat. She thought back to meeting Mr. Williams and how it was nothing and everything she had expected from such a session. She was glad her peers didn't know and ashamed to be the weak link in their chain. She guessed the group would not react well if they knew she had failed the initial assignment.

Ruby and Carlos were still talking privately in low tones, but they tuned in when Andy turned the interrogation back around on Sam. "What about you? You keep digging into other people's thoughts and what they have to bring to the table, but what about *you*? What ideas do you have for us?"

Each team member watched Sam, waiting for her response. She shook her head. Not yet. She had nothing to add. Instead, she focused attention back on Ruby.

"Your turn, Ruby Steffano." Sam pointed to Ruby with a lift of her chin and raise of her eyebrows. Challenge and determination sparkled in her eyes. "You're the acknowledged bomb-dot-com in teen culture. You have all the answers, right? Tell us how to do this project."

Ruby looked around at the team, at what she had to work with. She opened her mouth, then looked down and shook her head. She began again, eyes meeting Sam's first.

"Who said I know anything more about this than anyone else? I noted you didn't answer. You just passed the buck. So, tell us. What is love to you?" As the silence stretched on, she demanded: "Do we even have a definition?

Maybe we should start there. I mean, who really said we should know this stuff? Aren't we just kids?"

Jett nodded slowly and noted how postures relaxed at Ruby's declarations. She thought Ruby might be smart after all, still a Princess—but a smart Princess.

Ruby continued her soapbox speech, and the debate raged on. Each team member contributed definitions and examples of love. Finally, it was Jett's turn. She swallowed hard and buckled under the pressure of four peers waiting on her answer, waiting for her to explain love.

Uncharacteristically, she began to stutter. "I…I…I…I… oh…" Jett took a deep breath and twisted her hands. Knuckles white and body rigid, she held onto the jumble of ideas that wouldn't pass her lips. She could see the words she wanted to say, but they stayed locked inside. Then she remembered Ben. He had struggled to tell her about love, and he was a grown-up. Maybe they *weren't* qualified for this. Jett spoke under her breath. "This is ridiculous. I mean really, there should be a manual on how to be a loving person."

Sitting next to her, Ruby was the only one to hear Jett muttering to herself. "OhmiGAWD—Jett! I think you got it!"

Jett shrank in the unexpected heat of the spotlight.

Enthusiastically, Ruby yelled: "She got it! I think she got it!"

Carlos couldn't stand it any longer. "Linda, Cara, what? Jett got what?"

Ruby, suddenly remembering her group wasn't alone, drew them into a huddle, now whispering just loud enough for them to hear. "Jett said it first. We need a manual on how to be a loving person. I think we should create one. For reals. I mean, each of us sees it differently, so it's gonna take a lead to coordinate it all, to be in charge of how it all goes together. She can totally do that."

"You're in charge," announced Ruby, while turning towards Jett. "You can do that, right? You can put it all together and make the manual, right?"

Dumbfounded, Jett tried not to show her shock. Wow. This was not what she was expecting.

Ruby looked around for support, then pointed at Jett. "I mean, right? This Bug seems sharp and detail-oriented. She can handle this. Just give her your stuff." She waited for compliance.

The other team members, however, all seemed to check in with each other, without saying a word. Jett watched this transpire and wondered how they did that, and what it meant.

Again feeling like she was missing something, Jett was no longer sure she could handle the project on her own, especially because three-quarters of the entire grade for this class rested on this one assignment. She wondered what, exactly, the surreptitious looks between her teammates meant. At the risk of sounding stupid, she decided to see what she could find out. Avoiding eye contact as she continued to process what was happening, Jett started with Ruby.

"Okay, not sure how you decided the name 'Bug' means me, but my parents call me that sometimes, so I guess it just makes sense to others, even though I can't see why. I'll allow it *if* you give me all your data. I think we need to sort out how to be a loving person, so we have a strong hypothesis to test. Agreed? If we don't, what is our project worth? Any questions so far? Any suggestions? I want to know what love is, but you all seem to already know the answer. I took notes. So, let's jump straight to what we can actually measure: How do you *show* love?"

They all began speaking at once.

Jett looked from one teammate to another, trying to sort out who to listen to. It was impossible to make sense of anything in the chaos, so she jumped into the fray, speaking slowly, enunciating clearly, over-emphasizing each syllable. "Write. It. Down. Hand. It. Over. Go away."

Silence fell.

"Come on, guys. You heard her," Ruby said, taking charge. "Hand over whatever notes you have and your initial paper. She's got this. The Bug is gonna do her thing." Ruby winked at Jett and smiled.

Jett wondered if Ruby had something in her eye or had she really just winked on purpose? I mean, why would you wink after something like that? Jett shrugged, guessing that it didn't matter so long as her teammates were following directions. She had something to work with beyond her own meager notes. For a fleeting moment, she was excited as she collected their papers and notes before they left. Each smiled and thanked her as they handed their material over. That was odd, but refreshing.

And then she started to look over their notes. Not one of them had a decent hypothesis or strong supporting arguments. Really? She was supposed to work with this? These were the papers that passed when hers had failed? How? Suddenly, her head hurt. This just didn't make sense. Maybe she was missing something in the quick perusal. She would look more carefully when she got home and could start sorting things out on her project board. She put everything into her backpack and left, too.

At home, Jett looked at the notes she had stuck to her board on Love. She decided to try to incorporate their work into hers. Slowly, she began to feel better about helping her friends by taking charge and putting it all together. She could do this. They were trusting her because they were friends now, right?

Or was that right? Wait a minute. What about Ruby's wink? What about all the thank yous and smiles as they left? What if they were just using her to get a decent grade without putting forth a lot of effort? What if they made her feel special, like one of the team, just so they could use her for their own gain? Sam had warned her they weren't friends outside of class. Did that mean they were friends only when Jett spent time putting together their work, but not outside of class? Was she really so stupid?

Warring emotions battled inside her. Was she angry or overwhelmed or heartbroken? Was she glad they thought she could do the work, even though she knew she was the least qualified? She was the only one who had failed the initial assignment. Was she ashamed and feeling like she needed to prove her worth? Which of these? Could you have all at once? Because Jett thought she had all of these feelings and maybe more mixed up inside her. She wondered what to do with it all.

Just then, she flashed on Sam singing her pain, releasing it from her body through music. She decided to experiment with the idea and found songs to match her complex emotions. She spun around the room, jumped up and down, flapped her arms, and growled. She danced through it all. When calm enough to think it through, she brought her dance into the living room. Her tinny phone speakers weren't cutting it; Jett wanted the fuller range of a quality sound system.

Yes, that was better. "Coming Undone" was pounding through the house when suddenly she noticed her parents. She hadn't heard them arrive. In shock, Mother was watching Jett's dance of wild abandon. Eyebrows raised and a grin splitting his face, Daddio yelled, *"Yeah baby!"* and jumped right in. The music changed, and the party continued. In a nod to his old punk days, he raised his fists to the Gods of Rock and headbanged. Finally, her Mom jumped in and flailed around, happy to see Jett expressing herself to "Rebel Yell." And they all cried, *"more, more, more!"*

Yeah, this was not the day she had prepared for, nor were any of the reactions ones she predicted. Certainly, Jett had never seen this side of her parents, but she'd take it. Music really could break you and remake you.

13

ONE AFTERNOON, JETT was sitting on the campus lawn, categorizing the variation of autumn leaves. Soon winter break would be here, but for now she was happy with the new patterns emerging. She thought about the upcoming break. Too much free time. What would she do? Jett needed a plan. But now was not the time. She looked up when she heard Carlos and his cadre approaching.

Carlos and his teammates were crossing the lawn on campus, coming her way. Good. She needed to learn more from Carlos. To incorporate his data, she needed to know how he thought about love. She wondered about Sam's assertion that he saw it as a game, like soccer. Was this valid for him? She was curious. Would it be appropriate for her to speak to him outside of class? Were they friends right now? Jett couldn't resolve this without more information.

Carlos resolved the issue for her. "Hi, Jett!" he called out.

Relieved, she smiled. There you go. He called out to her. That answered that. They *were* friends outside of class. She stood and held up a hand in response. "Hi, Carlos! I'm glad to see you!"

Carlos bounded over, crew in tow. He held a soccer ball under his arm, tucked up against his hip.

Jett perused the small crowd of hangers-on. She didn't think they all played soccer, but most of them did. Some were girls from Ruby's crew, but the boys were all wearing something that identified them as athletes. They were studying her, too. She found it curious how others seemed to always watch peer interactions with fascination. Jett focused back on Carlos.

"I'm glad you said something. I have questions for you. Do you have answers?" Just in case his social skills were no better than Ruby's had been the other day, she tried asking permission before pursuing her inquiries about love, reasoning that this might help them avoid an awkward situation.

"Sure," he said. "What do you want to know?"

"So many things, Carlos. I feel you could tell me so many things."

Carlos looked around to ensure his guys were getting all of this. He looked pleased that she wanted him to tell her things, to be the expert.

"Okay, 'Manita. Shoot."

Jett's eyebrows lifted even as she tried to keep the surprise from her face. He got her name wrong and told her to shoot. Shoot what? She wondered if his brain injury would interfere with his answers, too. Would he actually be able to add to their team project? She decided to go easy on him and start with the basics, one question at a time. "Carlos, what is love?" Instead of answering, he looked around at his friends. She waited for his answer. She watched him look around again. Jett decided to prompt him with Sam's question. "Do you see love as a game, like soccer, with winners and losers, but hearts passed around instead of balls?"

Carlos was staring at her. This was very uncomfortable for her but Jett continued to try to engage him in the conversation. "You're a player, I know. But what happened with Ruby?"

That drew a collective "ooh" from his crowd. Had she asked something wrong? What had elicited that response? She didn't know. Carlos seemed frozen, so she decided to compliment him to see if that helped. "Carlos, I watched you try to talk to Ruby and help her understand things. I think you did the right thing. What I want to know is, do you love her? Will you teach me about love?"

Carlos dropped the ball and Jett watched as it rolled away. No one went after it. Strange. They all seemed rooted to the spot. Didn't they need the ball? Maybe they wanted to learn about love from Carlos, too. Huh. She had definitely asked the right questions, then. He could teach them all. She waited. She had done her best to engage him, but Carlos still seemed stunned.

Slowly, he shook his head as if coming out of a trance. "'Manita, no. No. No. No! I… " He looked around at his crew. "We need some privacy, guys. Go! My little sister and I need to talk." He put an arm around Jett, who shrugged him off.

Where was this Manita, his sister? She hadn't known he had a little sister.

Everyone stepped back except the guy standing to Carlos' right, who looked at Carlos avidly. "I can't help it," he said. "I want to know, too. Are you going to teach her about love? And what about your girl, Ruby?"

Carlos rolled his eyes, trying to push him away. "Hey, hey! Off me, man. Me and my sis, we got some things to discuss."

The guy stayed firmly planted, crossing his arms and settling in. "Okay, this ought to be good."

Carlos looked at Jett, who was waiting, but starting to fidget. She understood she was, yet again, missing something. Where was this little sister Carlos kept referring to? Why did he try to put his arm around her at the same time he was talking about… wait! Carlos must be having an episode. Did he not know she wasn't his little sister? Oh, no! How could she help him save face? How had he gone this far into the broken part of his brain without her recognizing it? Maybe he should stop playing soccer altogether; clearly, his injury wasn't healing and may even be getting worse. She needed to learn more about this, to do some research, maybe interview some experts. For now, though, she needed to help him. How could she do that?

As the silence grew too long, Jett consciously relaxed her posture. "Carlos, it's okay. Your friends can be here." The boy smiled triumphantly and gestured for the rest of Carlos' crew to step in closer as she explained her intent carefully. "You know, I just need to learn about love and I wanted to learn that from you. I wanted to know about Ruby, but maybe that is too much for you right now. It's okay, I can wait. I can be patient until you're done with—this." Jett gently put her hand on her temple, touching her head to let him know subtly that she knew about his brain injury, in case it wasn't public knowledge.

Carlos frowned. "What are you talking about, Jett?" He looked confused, but Jett was elated. He knew her name! He was back!

As the group moved in closer, eager to witness what promised to be an epic moment, Jett hoped they understood just how much this meant to her. She hoped Carlos wasn't upset like Ruby would have been. Did she fit the part here? She took internal inventory, deciding that her uniform of Keds, cuffed Levi's and a shirt chosen for comfort looked socially acceptable. The Madpax she touted everywhere set her apart; the Spiketus Rex was her signature piece.

Jett was confident that she looked the same as ever, even normal. Right?

She felt someone touching the backpack, though. She turned slowly, deliberately. The boy kept his hand on the bag. She looked him straight in the eye, hoping he felt the threat in her gaze, the censure for such an intrusive movement. When he moved his hand to caress her cheek, she reared back. How dumb is this guy? He didn't get it at all.

"Jett, is it? I can teach you about love. Carlos doesn't seem to know what to do. I do. I'll be nice. I can be gentle. What do you say?"

She stared at the stranger who was connected to her friend. This guy wasn't on their team. Did he think he could do Carlos' work to help him out?

Another boy stepped in front of the one who had touched her pack and reached for her face.

"Jett, pick me. I'll at least get to know you first," he said, elbowing the first intruder out of the way. "I know about love, and I have sisters. They would kick my ass if I didn't make it nice for you. We could start easy. Why don't we text a bit and see where it goes? What's your number?"

Wait. What? How would that... What did sisters have to do with it? Her mind was spinning. Yet another boy stepped up; Jett backed into Carlos. She'd momentarily lost sight of him while retreating from his crew. What should she do next? She thought about body language and the implied messages from postures. Although Carlos moved closer to her, this newest boy started talking to her. too.

"Hey, adorable Jett," he crooned. "Can I teach you about love? These bozos don't know as much as me, for sure. And I'm still friends with the others I've 'taught.'"

Carlos stepped in front of her, forcing the new boy back. "Guys. She doesn't *want* you. Stop. Seriously. Are you hitting on my 'Manita right in front of me?" He looked ready to fight. Jett found that interesting. She stood on tiptoes to see over the crowd of boys blocking her view. Maybe this 'Manita was coming her way and she just didn't see her yet. Who was hitting her? If she could see that, she knew what to do. She would run straight to the administration and let them know about the violence happening on their premises, maybe even call campus police while she was at it. Jett got ready to run.

Abruptly, she saw that the guys were closing off their body language, folding their arms across their chests and taking a step back in response to Carlos's challenge. Jett didn't see anyone moving to intercede on Manita's behalf, though. It seemed she was gonna have to run right through them to go get help. She pulled her backpack further onto her back, inserting the other arm through the strap. Her whole body tensed as she prepared to flee.

But Carlos was standing in the way. "Seriously?!? Look what you've done to her. Pobrecita. She is so *not* loving this. She's freaked out!" He widened his stance, drawing himself up to his full height. "Don't you understand? She is like my little sister! You guys just leave her alone or you are gonna have to answer to me! I mean it. Seriously." He looked each one in the eye as he caught a hold of Jett's arm before she could run. He took her hand and squeezed gently.

She let him.

Lowering his tone, he spoke soothingly just to her. "Jett, I've got you. Don't worry about these losers. Let's go. Together. Just us. I'll tell you everything I know. You want a hot chocolate? Let's go to the café." He looked over his shoulder and spoke a bit louder so the others could hear. "They won't follow. I've got you." And they left, hand in hand.

She felt torn as she continued to process everything since Carlos and his crew showed up. She needed his information about love for their project, but what about his little sister? Shouldn't they go to the authorities and enlist their help? Ensure punishment for the ones hurting her? She was so confused! She let Carlos lead her away.

Hot chocolate sounded so good.

14

JETT FELT PREPARED. An entire weekend spent studying traumatic brain injuries convinced her that she was right: Carlos may be severely impaired. She'd made an appointment to speak with Mr. Williams—that's where she was headed now. She didn't know who else to share her findings with. He seemed like a logical choice, and she hoped he took her seriously. She had prepared a 20-page paper with links to relevant research, articles, and experts. Jett was worried about Carlos, but also about Manita, the little sister she had yet to meet. Should she mention Manita to Mr. Williams? If younger, she probably didn't go to Presidio Prep. Yet. Would that matter if the crime against her person had happened on campus? She knocked on his door.

A moment later, Mr. Williams opened it and Jett passed through. She sat in the seat reserved for visitors, on the other side of the big mahogany desk. Battle scarred and worn, the large and sturdy workspace looked like it might be original to the first use of this space. Was it repurposed as well? That would be so cool.

Jett watched him return to his seat behind it. Definitely a new chair, made to look old but still new. It reminded her of the ones in Daddio's office. Covered in leather and traditional in style, the seat Mr. Williams occupied swiveled quietly towards her.

Leaning forward slightly, he faced her squarely. "Hello, Jett. First of all, congratulations on your second paper. Ms. Diaz told me she loved it. It was much more in line with what she expected."

Jett's eyebrows rose at this. *That* drivel? That *rant*? Was she even a qualified teacher?

Mr. Williams made eye contact and smiled. "I see you chose to seek me out. Knowing that, I expect whatever this is, it's important to you. What do you have for me?"

Jett liked his no-nonsense greeting, the way he didn't waste time with idle chatter. She appreciated his assessment that she would come to him with matters of importance. He did know her, maybe even better than her parents. That was a disturbing thought. She wondered how he knew so much from so few interactions. Would today change his opinion of her? What would he think when he learned that she knew things the staff had yet to catch, or that she had done nothing to protect Manita? No wonder her hands were involuntarily twisted together. She was shifting weight from side to side in an attempt to soothe herself. Jett felt him watching her.

"Would you like a seat? You could put your bag in the one right next to you for easy access, if you want."

Oh gosh. Maybe this wasn't a good idea. He was sharp. Too sharp. What if she lost the one ally she had here on campus? Her hands tightened on the strap she was unconsciously pulling at the bottom of her pack. White knuckles started turning red and Jett stayed standing.

"I think I need to go, Mr. Williams. This was a mistake. You might be offended or upset. What if what I tell you is important to me, but you don't see the importance? What if I did the wrong thing? What if my hypothesis is somehow faulty?"

The glasses magnifying Mr. Williams' eyes slid down his nose as he squinted at her. He pushed them back up. Had he been reading before she came into his office? He looked down at the open file sitting on top of his desk and closed it.

"Okay, Jett. First thing—let's take a breath." He breathed in audibly and she followed along, exhaling as he did.

They did it again. This was good. She liked breathing.

"Now, Jett. I need to tell you the truth. I may be offended." She took a step back. "I may be upset." She took another, but he held up his hand imploring her to wait. Jett squirmed but tried to stay put. "I may not reach the same conclusions from the information you share. But I assure you, I will not see it as of little importance."

Still tense, she intentionally unclenched the ends of her backpack strap. Did he notice the pulse of clench and release playing out in her jaw? Flexing her neck muscles to stop the rhythmic tic, she concentrated on staying still. Jett breathed in through her nose, smelling old books and new ink. She let out the breath she hadn't known she was holding, and settled.

"Now, please, take a seat. I've been looking forward to our time together ever since I saw it on my calendar."

She sat tentatively on the front of her seat; backpack still slung over one shoulder. Jett wasn't sure she made the right choice, calling him with her concern and making an appointment to speak about Carlos. Was it really any of her business?

Mr. Williams folded his hands across his lap, leaned back in his chair and placed his feet atop the desk he sat behind. He looked relaxed and unhurried.

That was a surprise. Was he allowed to put his feet on the desk? Wasn't that poor manners? Setting a bad example? After a long pause, Jett slowly unzipped her bag and pulled out her report. She wondered if he could see the internal battle she was fighting. Did she hand over the paper or make some excuse as to why she came? Jett handed over a copy of her report to him. "Mr. Williams, I think Carlos is in serious trouble. His little sister, too.

She's been hurt here on campus and I didn't do anything about it."

Eyebrows pinched, Mr. Williams leaned forward, tilted his head, and opened his mouth to speak. But nothing came out. He clamped his lips together and reached for his laptop to check something. "Mm-hmm. I see," he murmured. Turning back to her, he spoke soothingly. "We'll talk about the kind of trouble Carlos is in. But first, you should know that Carlos doesn't have a sister."

She was only half listening, distracted by the photos on his wall, but that brought her back to full attention. "Wait, what? Huh? Yes, he does. Her name is Manita. He said it three times in our recent conversation."

"You do mean Carlos from your Core5? Carlos Rodriguez? Because I double-checked his records just now and Carlos has no little sister. As for him being in trouble? It's possible, but he spends an extraordinary amount of time here on campus and I am surprised I haven't heard about it. Did you know he is the captain of the soccer team, even though he is only a freshman? That's unprecedented. I don't see how he could be into trouble without me becoming aware of it."

At least on this topic, on Carlos being in trouble, Jett felt she was on firmer footing. She nodded, since this confirmed her suspicions. No one else knew, which meant saving him was up to her. "Just to clarify? He isn't *into* trouble. He is *in* trouble. I actually doubt Carlos has the capacity to be into something nefarious. But he needs help and I don't believe the staff has picked up on it. I know he probably doesn't want anyone to know about it, but I also don't think it's fair to hold him to the same academic standards without accommodation. Also, I think he should quit soccer. Soccer could make this so much worse." She folded her arms across her chest. Jett had a case, a sound line of logic, and she was ready to fight for her friend. His entire life, at least his well-being, was at stake. She gestured towards the paper Mr. Williams now clutched without thought.

With his other hand, Mr. Williams rubbed at his forehead. His eyes never left the student in front of him. "Okay, Jett. You've caught my full attention. But I want you to know that our faculty are all highly attuned to anomalies. They would have caught any problem if it surfaced in their class. Please explain to me what you know. I want to hear you out."

She started a lengthy monologue about Carlos's inferior ability to assess data. As he glanced through her paper, she gave him all the relevant information stored in her brain and how she came to her conclusion. By the time she was done, Mr. Williams was leaning halfway over his desk, chin resting on his hand. As she wrapped up, Jett took off her pack, set it in the chair next to her, and sat back. She was exhausted but keenly aware. Jett waited for him to signal if he was angry or grateful. She couldn't read his body language.

Finally, he sat back with a smile on his face—but Mr. Williams was shaking his head in denial, at the same time. This was so confusing. Why was he smiling *and* shaking his head? People were just so … so … unclear.

"Wow, Jett. Just—wow. I'm not sure where to begin. You are a wonderment and a powerhouse. Has anyone ever told you that?"

Now she was the one shaking her head.

"Have you ever considered your attention to detail, your ability to recall conversations and reconstruct events as a superpower? Also, I love how you research and put things together. I love how you are so deeply caring for others. I don't think many know that about you, do they?"

She shrugged. How would she know what others knew?

"I'm gonna need a minute. And while I'm thinking this all the way through, I want you to know you are so right, even when you are wrong."

Wait. What? Right when wrong? What the heck? It felt like he was deliberately trying to confuse her. Either he didn't understand English very well or she didn't. How could you be right when you are wrong? Arms crossed protectively against her chest, Jett waited. This ought to be good.

"Also, from what you just shared I think I figured out who he called Manita. I can solve that one for you."

Gripping the base of her seat but sitting tall and slightly forward, she thought that this was the strangest twist in a conversation she'd ever heard. Jett didn't know what to expect next. "Okay." She clasped her hands on her lap to stop their unconscious tapping at the underside of her chair.

"Let's start with your assertion that his brain is foggy because he mislabels things, especially people. He calls Ruby 'Linda.' Did you know *linda* means beautiful in Spanish? I think he's calling her Linda on purpose. As for Manita? It's also a term of endearment. He could be saying 'little hand' or a shortened form of 'little sister.' The full term you would learn in Spanish class would be *hermanita* but in everyday slang, sometimes people say *'manita*. Do you now know who he was referring to? Think over the last exchanges again, Jett."

She thought for quite a while, running the memories through her head as if they were a movie scene. Suddenly, her jaw dropped. As she looked at Mr. Williams, she realized her mouth was hanging open. She shut it as she saw him smile and nod at her.

"Mm-hmm. Carlos has decided to call you Manita. To him you are like a little sister. He has made that clear. Do you see that? Do you understand?"

With lips clamped shut and her face registering the implications, Jett blinked rapidly. "I see that, but I don't understand. I mean, we're peers. I'm smaller than he is, but by no means his little sister. We come from different families. We're not even from the same side of the Bay. I can see why he would call Ruby beautiful. That is a fact—she is. But Carlos calling me 'little sister'? How does this make sense? I don't see any supporting facts."

Mr. Williams spent the next several minutes trying to explain what Carlos could mean by using this term of endearment for her. Jett shook her head until she gave in, frowning. Did she really have a choice? She decided to allow it, for her friend's sake. Jett wasn't convinced Carlos was right in the head. Why make his life harder?

"All right, I'll accept it. But Mr. Williams, why don't people just say precisely what they mean? Do you know how much room for misinterpretation is left when people don't have the same definitions or constructs to work from? How will we understand each other? And wait a minute—are you implying Carlos may *not* have a traumatic brain injury? Are you saying he doesn't need accommodation for his disability? Are you saying he's naturally this ... this ... " She threw her hands in the air, incredulous. "Are you trying to tell me Carlos is naturally this way?"

After letting out a huge breath, his whole body relaxed. Mr. Williams smiled in reassurance. "Jett, you may just be the smartest student at this school."

Jett looked him in the eye and nodded solemnly. "I know."

His mouth twitched. "And do you also know being smartest is *not* the most important reason we need you to keep working with us?"

Jett grunted. "Do you know Spiderman? Uncle Ben is my favorite because he was the best but I wish he had gotten it right. With great *knowledge* comes great responsibility."

"Well, knowledge *is* power..." A twinkle lit his eyes, as Jett continued to charm him.

"Can I ask you about something else? Something I learned from my teammate, Sam? Sam told me some things that make sense but also don't. Can you tell me how the timing of 'friends' works? Do you know how to tell which friends are friends inside or outside of class only, or both? And have you thought about who my peer role models should be? If you don't know, maybe they do."

Mr. Williams stared at her.

She felt like he was looking into her soul. Expectation and duty weighted the silence.

"Jett, I wish I had a simple answer for this. I wish I could tell you the schedule. I wish I could dismiss the very real and very complex unspoken rules of society—but I can't. I'm afraid you're going to have to sort that one out, as well as your role models, without anyone handing you the knowledge. When you pick some people, let me know and I can tell you if any one of them are troublemakers not worthy of your time right now. But you need to be the one to make those choices."

Absorbing this, she nodded. "Okay, Mr. Williams. I'm good at learning. Do you think this is something I could learn over winter break if I put my research skills to use? Will this help people know I am normal?"

"I don't know. What I do know is you *aren't* normal." The Counselor waited until he was sure Jett was meeting his eyes.

It took a while. She didn't like hearing she wasn't normal, especially from Mr. Williams.

When her eyes finally met his, he finished the thought. "Jett, you are exceptional!"

Instinctively and in a very small voice, she protested. "But what if I don't want to be?" Jett stared into his eyes and tried again, pleading. "What if I don't want to be exceptional? What if I want to be normal?"

His face softened. "I don't think you have a choice in that."

She looked down, thinking of Mother. Jett wished "normal" was as easy for her as "exceptional" obviously was. Maybe then she would be lovable.

The door to his office opened. Startled, they both looked up. Principal Fujita waved her hand apologetically. "Excuse me, Counselor," she said. "I didn't know your appointment was still here. Are you ready for our weekly meeting?"

Mr. Williams looked to Jett for confirmation. She nodded slightly and rose to leave.

"Um, yes. Is it really that time already? I'll be there shortly."

As Ms. Fujita closed the door again, he returned his focus to Jett. "I believe you have a pivotal role in Presidio Prep. Have a wondrous winter break, Jett Harper. I look forward to receiving your update in the new year."

Pulling her bag onto one shoulder, she struggled to balance the weight. So much knowledge and so much yet to learn. She fought to steady herself, straightening her spine, squaring her shoulders, and dropping her fingers off the strap of her backpack as she turned to go. Overwhelmed, Jett walked out alone.

15

JETT WASN'T COUNTING the days towards Hanukkah, even though it meant latkes, laughter, and eight days of presents. Nor was she counting the days until Christmas, which would be recognized with more gifts and traditions. In her home, they did all these things, and to Jett, it just didn't hold a speck of importance compared to time with Yoda. Winter break and she couldn't wait for longer days to play with him.

Yoda! His training was coming along so nicely. Every afternoon for the last few months, they had gotten to spend some time together. Ben even let her walk Yoda or play with him by herself once in a while. Time with this furry companion truly was the bright spot in her life. She couldn't wait for lots more time, unencumbered by school and pressing responsibilities.

Jett wondered if she could make a deal with Ben so she could even have Yoda overnight. Maybe she could persuade him to do it as a gift to her. She'd have to ask her parents first, of course. But maybe Ben would like the break. Which winter holiday did he celebrate? Would he let her take Yoda then?

Wait. Presents. Should she get gifts for Yoda and Ben? Was that expected? Appropriate? Being 14 was so awkward sometimes. It was hard to know the rules, what was expected, and what was exceptional. Hearing Yoda bark once, intentionally, like he was calling to her, her brain abruptly stopped spinning. It was time to take a break.

She looked out the window. Sure enough, Yoda was staring in at her. His tail looked like it might seriously hurt someone if they stepped into the path of its frantic waving.

Jett held back a laugh. Looks like she and Yoda were on the same page. She needed time with Yoda and he wanted time with her. Now to get Ben to agree.

She skipped to the front door, threw it open wide and, in her best dramatic voice, she bellowed: "Hello, World! It's winter break and I'm ready to rumble!"

Yoda's waving picked up the pace. "Looks like my favorite sidekick is ready, too!" Jett declared. "Hello, Yoda! Are you ready to sniff out adventure?"

The puppy came bounding over, but Ben was in his own world. Failing even to look up from what he was doing, he missed her unusual antics. Instead, he looked intent on—packing his car? Why was all his attention on that? She stared toward Ben, willing him to join them.

He didn't.

What was going on? This made no sense. Why hadn't he even cracked a smile at her over-the-top antics? Wait—was he crying? There were tears streaming down his face. Was he laughing? Was she that funny?

No. Those were sad tears—devastated, or frustrated, or heartbroken tears—not happy, joyful, ridiculously funny tears.

Why was he packing his car? Enough was enough. She decided to ignore all the incongruencies she didn't understand. He must be having what her Father called a "Hallmark Moment." Jett knew this phrase well because her mother always cried during Hallmark movies, sometimes even just after the commercials. Even her Dad cried, sometimes. She had seen this. But she didn't understand. Jett decided to try again with the rhyme greeting she had made up just for him.

"Ben, my friend! What's a-happenin' on your end?" She waited for a return rhyming response, but he was silent. Hunh. Maybe her cadence was off. At least it had the effect of getting him to notice her. She reached for Yoda and waited expectantly for his reaction. Jett blinked seven times while waiting.

Ben seemed to be struggling even to look her in the eye, much less to greet her in the exuberant way she had approached him. Ultimately, he gave up and started crying all over again. "Oh, Jett. Oh, my. I can't..." Then he crumpled to the ground.

Usually, she loved that he was so enthusiastic, so dramatic. He reminded her of Carlos. But Jett wasn't loving it now. Yoda was standing watch next to him, guarding against this unseen danger. But what was she supposed to do? How did she handle a grown man curled up on the ground?

Jett felt Yoda waiting for her to *do* something and wondered what he expected. "Um, Ben? Should I maybe call someone? I see you are packing your car, but I am not sure you should drive right now. What are your plans? Where are you going? For how long? Is anyone expecting you? Maybe we should call them? I can take Yoda while you're gone. Also, are you done crying? Can you get up? I'm not sure Yoda's ready to witness such an emotional outburst."

The puppy started licking at his tears and Jett was disgusted. "Gross! Why is he doing that? And how come you're letting him?"

Ben threw his arms around Yoda and just sobbed harder. It was the saddest thing she'd ever seen. Tentatively, she put a hand on his shoulder. She liked when her father did that when she was upset, just putting a light hand on her shoulder and waiting for her to choose what she wanted to share.

"Oh, Jett! I didn't know it would be like this! I thought I could handle it. For goodness' sake, Yoda didn't even have a name until recently. How can this hurt so much?"

"What hurts, Ben? Where are you in pain? Shall I call 911? It looks like an emergency."

He shook his head and gulped as he tried to calm himself.

"Should I call my mom, then? She'll know what to do."

Again, he shook his head.

She decided to take a further lesson from how her father had handled unexpected situations. "Okay, Ben. We'll just figure this out together, then. Tell me what's going on. How can I help?"

Ben was using Yoda's presence to soothe himself. He sat with Yoda's front legs and half his body draped over him like a blanket. Ben's hands rhythmically stroked Yoda's fur as if he was memorizing every inch of the dog. She was fascinated.

"What are you doing? What's happening? I think Yoda really likes this. Can you teach me? I want to try it when I walk him next."

Ben started crying all over again, but this time with some control. "But Jett! This is it. Yoda has to go with me. I'm taking him to school."

Oh, so *that's* what the problem was! She was relieved to have some clarity.

"Okay, but you've been working toward this," she said as soothingly as she could. "Yoda is going to school and that's a good thing. Right? It's what you've been training for. It sucks that he starts school during my break, but I can spend all my time with him when he gets back each day. When will he come home? Do you know the timing yet? Will he take a special bus or something? I can be here to meet him if you're busy. And I'm guessing he'll have weekends off so that won't interrupt our usual routine."

Ben swallowed. Hard. A lump in his throat made it impossible to speak and he shook his head several times, trying to dislodge the lump, so he could speak.

"No, Jett," he croaked softly. "No. You don't..." And then the crying resumed.

Jett crossed her arms. She was losing her patience with all this.

"Ben, look at me." She wanted him to see how his histrionics were affecting her. "I'm sorry to admit this, but I'm getting exasperated. You said 'no.' No—what? At least tell me that. What are you crying about? Seriously. This isn't a Hallmark movie. This is life, and I don't understand why you're so upset. It's not like you didn't know Yoda was going to school eventually. All puppies grow up. Did you know I just called out a rhyme I made for you? You didn't even respond. That's so not like you. Tell me what's going on."

"That's just it, Jett," he said, finally sitting up but keeping Yoda firmly on his lap. "I guess I didn't explain it as well as I thought I did." Ben took a deep breath, held it for a moment, and then let out a long exhale. "Jett, Yoda is going to school, like, a boarding school—and he's not coming back."

"Wait. *What?!?*" Her heart felt frozen in her chest as she watched Ben slowly stand up and face her.

"He's going to school to learn how to help someone, how to be of service, how to assist. I'm just his puppy raiser. Hopefully, I've done a good enough job that he'll get a job. He'll get a new partner who will love him and need him, and I won't see him. *We* won't.

"This is goodbye."

Jett stared open-mouthed. She felt her own face do that fish thing, trying to breathe. Open. Close. Open. Close. She kept trying to breathe. It was hard. Slowly she bowed her head and looked at Yoda, who was standing between them now, watching their conversation for clues on who was going to play next. She turned away slowly.

"No. Ben, you have this wrong. This is not what we discussed. This isn't how friends work. They don't just pack up, move away, and you never hear from them again."

Yoda sidled up to her and put his nose under her dangling hand. She didn't respond. Shock held her captive as she tried to process losing the brightest spot in her life. She stared wordlessly into the distance.

Ben watched her, tears flowing down his cheeks again. "I'm sorry, Jett. It didn't occur to me how much I didn't tell you about this program. This is how it works. I need to take him to his school now. Did you want to say goodbye?"

Yoda pushed up into her palm again, eager to get her attention. But Jett just couldn't. Feeling the weight of the loss, she was afraid to bond with him any more than she already had. Did he know? Did Yoda understand this was it? This was goodbye? Forever? No more tug-of-war games, no more walks together, no more playing ball or getting treats for tricks?

She started to move as if waking from a trance. She couldn't do this. She wouldn't do this. She backed up one step. Then two. Three. Four. She pivoted and ran like her worst nightmare was chasing her.

Ben called after her. "Jett. Jett! Wait! I... Wait, Jett!"

But she was gone.

16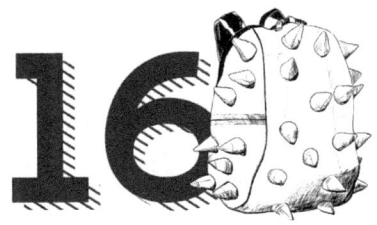

JETT FELT BLOOD coursing through her veins. Her body was overheating. She was sweaty and sticky, soggy and stymied. If this is what it felt like to be a runner, why did anyone do it on a regular basis, *especially* on purpose? She hadn't run deliberately before and now she was paying the price. Her heart was beating out of her chest. *Is this what a heart attack felt like?* She was tired of running. The distance she had flown without conscious thought was more than she would have imagined. Her body felt like it wasn't under her control. She might just pass out. Finally her steps began to slow, but she couldn't discern why.

She was feeling too much. Jett wanted no part of it. Maybe that's why people ran. Emotional turmoil propelled them, and they had to. That she could understand. What she couldn't wrap her brain around was Yoda leaving and not coming back. Tears threatened to overflow. She swallowed hard, blew out a breath, and watched it stream out in front of her. It was so cold she could see her breath, but she had to keep going. Jett hadn't yet outrun the pain. She had to get away.

Slowly coming back to awareness, Jett completed the last few steps into the Strawberry Village Shopping Center. Maybe a jolt of sugar would help her system. She debated whether to turn to ice cream or hot chocolate. It was winter, but she had just run for her life. Yeah, ice cream it was.

As a lifelong regular at the shop, she expected the greeting from the kid behind the counter. He looked taller and more gangly than she remembered, either a giraffe like Andy or a puppy like Yoda. He must be growing, too. "Hey, Jett. Your usual? Or did you want to try the egg nog ice cream today? On account?"

"Yes, the usual, please." She could feel her heartbeat still drumming in her veins, throbbing at her temples, pulsing in her fingertips. She was sure she was bright red. Sweat pasted her hair to her head. So gross. Did he notice? He didn't seem to notice. She needed a distraction, not only from the trauma of being left but also from the trauma of her body in this state. "Can I ask you a question?"

He kept his eyes on the ice cream scoop. "Sure. What's up?"

"Can you tell me how you experience love?"

Jett watched his reaction for signs of distress. She had recently begun to recognize that sometimes people didn't like to talk about love. His body language hadn't tensed.

He actually paused for a moment and then seemed to relax. She guessed it was okay to have asked.

"Wow, Jett. What a beautiful question. Let me think about it for a moment." He handed her the ice cream in a cup with the sugar cone on top, just the way she liked it, then passed her a spoon before wiping his hands on his apron.

"I think I experience love when my buddies come to get ice cream, when they take the time to come see me while I'm working and they're all hanging out together. Know what I mean?"

Jett nodded and then shook her head. "Yes, I think I do, but maybe not. Can you give me another example?"

"Sure. Yeah. Okay. I feel loved when..." He looked off into the distance. After his eyebrows furrowed then rose, he refocused on her. "I feel loved when customers ask me questions that show they're interested in me, not just my ice cream."

She tilted her head. Did he feel loved by her? How was this possible? Jett didn't love him, not on purpose. She still wasn't sure she loved anyone. Should she correct him? No. Perhaps she should let him stay delusional; maybe receiving love was more important than being right. Maybe his getting love mattered more than her knowingly giving it. She nodded slowly. "Thank you. That's a lot to think about, valuable information." Jett took a bite and turned to go. "I'll see you soon."

Wandering outside, she saw a lady walking her dog. Immediately her mind went to Yoda's departure and her whole body tensed. The lady had a ball on a rope, and she was playing with her dog as they walked. She looked like she loved him/her/it? Wow. A lot. They were both radiating something—happy. Was that joy? They were coming her way. Jett froze. Should she warn the lady how much it will hurt when *her* dog went away? Should she let the lady know? Wouldn't that be loving? Was Jett a loving person? She shook her head. She couldn't do it. She was not loving.

Jett inhaled and looked down at her phone. She couldn't handle it, a person and their dog playing, while Yoda was leaving. She had to get out of here. She had to go before the woman and her dog reached her. Jett called herself a ride through the app Mother had installed on her phone. Within minutes, the car was there to pick her up.

After matching the license plate and description to the data in the app, she opened the rear door.

"Are you Jett?"

The driver reminded Jett of a cunning and wily fox. She wasn't sure how she felt about that. She had expected someone more like a sea otter, happy-go-lucky and just here for adventure. This guy was muscular and compact, but powerful and assured. He looked well kept and carefully put together, one of those drivers who thought to have small bottles of water and chargers available for his passengers. She checked his car data once again. Yes, a white Prius with a license plate matching her notes. He was her driver this trip. Still, a fox and an otter were very different creatures and Jett had to rearrange her thinking.

"Yes. I am Jett Harper," she said, following the script Mother had taught her for speaking with strangers who drove her when she was alone. "I am not good with idle conversation and I am very happy to have silence. I also don't like the windows down. Can you please take me safely to my destination under these conditions?"

The man turned all the way around. His short auburn hair was not even long enough to react to the breeze coming through the window as he rolled it up. He inspected her. Jett had found this was a typical reaction. Either the driver would turn around and stare at her or peek at her in their rearview mirror. Men tended to stare. Women peeked.

"Sure," he said with a friendly smile. "I can do that." But he shook his head as he turned back towards the front of the car. This shaking of his head was incongruent, but also something she had learned to predict. Nothing unusual for her here, other than taking a ride to somewhere other than school or home. They traveled in silence.

Jett stared out the window as they crossed the Golden Gate Bridge. Soon they were wending their way along the bluffs to the south. When he pulled up to Baker Beach, he turned to speak to her, but she held up her hand to stop him.

"Thank you very much for the ride. Your services are appreciated. Travel safely and have a good day." She hopped out of the car, shut the door, and immediately started walking to the beach.

The crash of the waves expanded in her chest. She felt the rumble. This was what she had needed. The symbolism was spot on. Jett surrendered to the mercy of the moment. She had held herself together for far too long. And, this was exactly what she needed, to feel the thudding surf on the sand, to hear the roar of the ocean drowning out the cry of her heart. She breathed in deep and shuddered as she exhaled. Jamming her earphones into place, Jett put on her "pain" playlist and let her body sway with the weight of her grief. She turned the soundtrack way up and tried deep breathing again, but this time when she exhaled she felt tears running down her face as she gave in to a deep, shuddering sob. With a low, guttural moan, she collapsed, burying her hands in the sand. It wasn't fair. She cried more. Her mind kept returning to Yoda—leaving. Left. Gone. She cried and cried. On her face, salty tears joined the ocean spray.

It couldn't be true. Yoda had to come back. Had he even been to the beach yet? Jett felt like she was breaking inside. Was this love, this visceral pain of losing someone you counted on? And if it was, why did people want it so much? Didn't they know it could wreck you? This was too much. All her plans for winter break? Erased. What was she supposed to do now? She needed another distraction.

She looked around and saw two people, a couple, being filmed by someone; someone a little ways off who wasn't part of their moment. This put her on alert. She turned off her playlist. How was that okay? Did they know their privacy was being violated, that this moment, this potential memory, was being captured on film? Should she warn them? Jett stood up and brushed herself off. Maybe she should tell them. They didn't seem to be aware of anything but each other. Was that love? Maybe they could tell her. She started walking towards them, but stopped abruptly as the man went down on one knee while the lady had her back turned, taking in the Golden Gate Bridge. She watched the lady turn back around and put a hand to her mouth. This looked like a real live Hallmark movie. Maybe filming was appropriate after all. Jett walked to the videographer and tapped him on the shoulder. "Excuse me," she whispered.

He held up a finger and continued filming. As Jett waited, the couple looked up towards the one capturing this memory. Oh, good. They *did* know. Phew. Jett didn't have to intercede. The couple came towards them.

"Hi, hi, hi! OhmiGAWD—did you know? Of course, you knew! I just thought we were getting pictures taken together. Did you know?" The lady flashed a new ring on her left hand as she gushed.

The man beside her beamed joyfully and stuck out his hand to shake the photographer's. "Hey, man, thanks!

That was epic!" He looked towards Jett and back to the videographer. "Looks like you picked up an assistant."

The trio turned towards Jett, who just shrugged. It was now or never. "I'm doing a project on how humans experience love. Would you mind telling me about how you experience love, for my data collection?"

Now all three were grinning. Knowing they had something to share, Jett was waiting, trying to stay focused.

Unexpectedly, a wet and sandy goldendoodle barreled into her. She lost it. As Jett fell back, arms flailing, she began to shout. "No, no, no! I can't. No, no! I don't. *No!*"

Once again, she found herself running. Jett felt their eyes on her back as she heard someone call out. It didn't matter. She had to run. Jett took off. Jamming her earbuds back in, she started up her "sad songs" playlist. She thought about playing the "angry" playlist, but it wasn't quite time. Anger would come. It usually followed sadness, but she had to get through sad to find her angry. Still running, she soon found herself on a trail heading toward her school.

She stopped at the overlook to breathe, seeing the beautiful bridge stretched out before her and wondering how long it would take to get home. The sun was setting soon and she knew pedestrians weren't allowed on the Bridge at night. Jett started to run again, faster than ever, racing the twilight. She prayed she'd beat the setting sun, knowing she didn't have much time.

Gasping for breath, Jett didn't stop running until she got to the statue of the Lonely Sailor. She had made it across the Bridge, at least. She turned up her music volume without looking down, missing the low battery notification. It turned itself off before the current song even finished. Her phone had run out of juice. Now what was she gonna do? She couldn't call for a ride and home was further away than she had ever walked before. Plus, it was dark now.

Did her parents know she wasn't home? Were they back from work yet? She remembered that they had planned to be home early to celebrate the completion of her first high school semester. Jett's body had taken that information away from her when it decided to flee the pain. Would she be in trouble? How could she get home quickly and safely?

Jett looked up into the face of the lonely sailor until the fading light erased his expression. She sat down at his feet to think this through. Did she even know how to do this? How to walk home and not walk on the freeway? There must be a way. Maybe she could find a map posted nearby. This was one end of the Golden Gate Bridge for goodness sake!

A strong, deep voice ended her internal debate. "Excuse me, young lady."

In the gathering gloom, she could just make out a pair of boots—Highway Patrol regulation boots, to be exact. The officer's feet looked big. She looked up—and up. He *was* big, and he was talking to her. There was no one else around.

He was a stranger, but he *was* a police officer, wasn't he? Should she answer, even though he was a stranger? Jett gave him the benefit of the doubt.

"Yes, sir?"

"Can you tell me what you are doing here, alone, in the dark, and without a winter coat? Where are your parents?"

"I am sitting here, alone, in the dark, without a winter coat because I didn't need it when I left. I don't know where my parents are at this moment, but it is safe to assume they are at home."

The officer took a step back as he studied her. Jett watched him assess her well-being. She knew that look. He couldn't tell what to do with her. Well, join the club. It was tough being her. If Mr. Williams was right, she wasn't normal, but she was exceptional. Would the officer see this? Weren't officers supposed to be helpful?

They stared at each other until the officer broke the silence. "How did you get here? Do you need help?"

Face screwed up with concerted effort, Jett tried to look deep into his face. She tried to assess her best course of action. She did need help. He was an officer. Her phone was dead. Jett was going to have to trust him. Somewhat.

"Yes, sir. I do need help. Can you please drive me to Tiburon? I can't get my ride app to work and I need to get home." She intentionally didn't mention her battery was dead. She might look too vulnerable if he knew she couldn't be traced.

"All right. That makes sense." He smiled at her.

This made her more anxious, not less. Why did she have to run away? Why couldn't she have asked Ben to take her along to see Yoda's school and give him a good send off? Ben probably would have liked her company. Why hadn't she thought of that?

Her mind returned to the officer's strange reaction. With so little information, she couldn't see how any of this made sense, but at least he was willing to help her. Jett would have to make sure she remembered his name and badge number for her father. She told him her address, feeling glad to be going home. She was exhausted. Right now, all she wanted was her cozy bed and a warm mound of blankets.

17

AS THEY PULLED into her cul-de-sac, Jett saw chaos. A policeman stopped them and the two officers spoke to each other using some sort of numbered code. A flashlight pointed directly into her face and the one outside nodded before speaking into his earpiece. Something big was going on, but she was too tired to care—until her Highway Patrol driver addressed her.

"Young lady, Higgins will take you the rest of the way home. I need to get back to my route." He lifted two fingers in a wave or salute of some sort. She couldn't be sure.

Practicing her best Ruby impression, she nodded at him in dismissal, then turned her attention to the new officer, who had moved to stand beside her open window. Didn't this guy have something more important to do than escort her? She could get home from here. She tried telegraphing her dissatisfaction, pursing her lips, then staring and squinting at him, but he didn't relent. Instead, he opened her door and gestured for her to exit. Jett was too tired to argue.

He stayed beside her as they approached the confusion. That's when she realized that the chaotic craziness was centered on *her* home base. Jett looked around trying to make sense of it all, to see the anomalies and piece it together. But she couldn't, because it didn't make sense. Not to her.

She held up a hand and took a step back, knowing she hadn't been spotted. Everyone was lost in their own intense moment and that gave her a minute to watch. Jett put a finger to her lips and glanced at Higgins so the officer would know she wanted silence. He shrugged and looked on curiously.

Her parents and Ben stood together awkwardly on her front porch. Anger radiated off them. Stiff body language emphasized the tense scene before her; Jett knew that look. Mother was ramping up for one of her infamous lectures. Poor Ben. Poor Daddio. She wanted to hear this before drawing attention to herself so that she would know what she was walking into.

"I'm sorry, but who exactly are you and what do you know of our daughter?"

Her mother's tone was awful. Was she really speaking to Ben—her Ben—like that?

Jett saw Bens' eyes go wide as he shifted his gaze to her Dad. Even Daddio had his chest raised and arms crossed in his perfected prosecutor's pose. Ben wasn't finding any sympathy there. Both her parents were staring at him like he was the enemy.

"I've already explained this," he said, clearing his throat. "I saw Jett earlier today. She was upset and I saw her take off."

"Excuse me. Did you say she was upset? What makes you draw this conclusion?" Daddio asked. "You do know our daughter is *always* composed, right? For a girl of her age, she's unusually collected. Jett never 'just takes off.' What provoked her?"

Mother didn't wait for his answer. "Did you?" she accused him. "Did you say or do something to cause her to run away?"

Ben looked stunned and a man Jett didn't recognize stepped in.

"Ben, this is Detective Ian Choate," her dad said. "You don't mind if he joins our conversation, do you?"

Suddenly Ben was doing his fish impression, trying to capture air, as he opened and closed his mouth several times in rapid succession. Jett knew he did that when he didn't know what to say. She listened as Ben explained about Yoda and his relationship to her. He was doing great, Jett thought. She wondered how her parents didn't already know all of this, suddenly realizing that they usually were at work when she spent time outside with Ben and Yoda.

The detective took notes while Mother became increasingly agitated. "You mean to tell me she just took off and you *let* her? Seeing her distress, you did *nothing* to stop her?!? What kind of man are you? What were you thinking? How could you be so irresponsible? Anything could be happening to our baby girl and if so, it will be your fault," she said, thrusting a pointed talon of a finger into Ben's face. "If anything happens to her, it's all your fault!"

Jett saw Ben's face drain of color as she felt her own posture go rigid. This couldn't be happening. Was Mother *really* insinuating that Ben somehow was responsible for her? Wait—was he *hired* to spend time with her? She thought their meetings were random, that Yoda had brought them together. Jett felt her heart breaking all over again. She watched Ben's jaw flex as he sized them up, ready to explode.

"Yes, anything could be happening to her. Or not. Either way, you are her parents, not me, and I take no responsibility for her whereabouts. I was neither asked to engage nor paid to watch after her. Good luck, lady," he said as he turned to Jett's dad. "Sir, I am sorry for your pain. I hope she returns healthy and whole and *soon*. She is too kind, thoughtful, and decent for the likes of *her*," he finished, jabbing a finger at Jett's mother before marching down the stairs.

That's when he saw her. A lone tear rolled down Jett's cheek. His eyes watered and overflowed, too. He let out a breath that sounded like it had been held inside for far too long.

"Oh, Jett," he choked out. "I'm so sorry, chum. I can see why you're so glum." He walked toward her, but suddenly Mother saw her, and no one else was allowed near.

With arms waving frantically, Mother came barreling at her. "Jett! Jett! Oh, thank you, Lord. She's here! Right here!" She looked at the officer and nodded in dismissal. But she only had eyes for Jett.

"Where have you been? What happened?" She grabbed her daughter by the arms and didn't wait for a reply, nor for permission, as she pulled Jett into an embrace and didn't let go.

Jett was caught by surprise. What was happening? She was trying to process as she stood smothering in Mother's embrace. No one seemed to notice. She waited to be released, but remained captive. How was this okay? Jett counted silently, wishing she knew how long she should put up with this. Mother said that each person was in charge of her own body. Was there some kind of exception Jett didn't know about? She needed the rules.

Barely holding it together, she realized that her system was overloading. This confrontation was not what she wanted. Still, she didn't say a word. Over and over, Mother had drilled into her that no one could touch her without her permission. Why, then, was Mother allowed to violate that edict? This was out of line and yet Jett felt that she couldn't speak up.

At long last, Mother pushed back to hold Jett at arms' length. "Honey, where have you been? What happened? Are you okay? Seriously, I tried calling and you didn't pick up. You always pick up. Then, you weren't home and … " Her voice trailed off in confusion.

Jett huffed and her eyelids drooped. She was just so tired. It was all too much. Didn't Mother realize Yoda wasn't home and wouldn't be coming back? Why was she still clinging onto her?

Mother steered her into the house, where there were more strangers, some of them photographing and cataloguing things, as if they were on one of those TV crime shows. Mother started herding her towards her room, when out of the corner of her eye she saw a stranger touching her research, messing with her work. Jett ducked under her mother's arm and made a beeline to the rumpled man in an ill-fitting suit studying her data. She felt rage welling up inside. *What the actual —*

This peculiar person was touching—and *photographing!*—all of her carefully collected and catalogued data. She felt the violation like a physical blow. Jett wasn't ready to share it even with her Core5 and now someone she'd never even seen before had it. What if this stranger used her work as his own? Daddio must have had him sign a nondisclosure agreement; maybe he just hadn't had a chance to tell her yet. He wouldn't let thieves into their home. Jett wasn't so sure about Mother, though. Mother seemed to trust these complete strangers entirely.

Mother's voice, molded into a pacifying cadence, interrupted her thoughts.

"Jett, it's okay," she said, waving dismissively at these thieves. "It's all fine. I mean, not everything you've put up there is fine, but I told them they could take pictures of everything."

Jett backed away from her. Okay? *Okay!?!* Of course Mother didn't mind. It wasn't *her* intellectual property being stolen and copied. Who was she to give permission? Would she allow this casual violation of her patient files, let them take pictures of all *that* data? What if Jett gave these busybodies carte blanche to paw through Mother's work? Would they steal that, too? Ruin more lives?

This violation of trust was unforgivable. She was bereft. In a single afternoon, she had lost Yoda. She lost Ben. And now she was expected to stand here watching as she lost her work and her privacy. Jett was done with being violated. She wouldn't stand for it. She turned and walked back out of the house.

"Jett, where are you going? Answer me! Jett! Stop right there and speak to me. Stop this nonsense! I am your Mother!"

Jett stopped. She opened her mouth, wanting to say something—anything—to make Mother understand. Jett had so much to say, but she couldn't manage a single word of it.

Mother stood frozen, watching Jett walk out. Was it rage, indignation, or a blend of both, that held her in place?

"Ma'am? I'm sorry to interrupt but we have a few more questions."

Fed up with the histrionics, Jett was grateful for whomever detained Mother. She walked toward Ben's stoop even though it was late. She knew he was inside. Jett hoped he would look outside, see her sitting there, and join her. She waited, but Ben didn't come out.

As the minutes passed, she started to sort through the debris leftover from all of the drama. Jett started to plan, taking notes into her phone. It was a soothing ritual.

1) *get Ben to talk*
2) *find out exactly where Yoda is*
3) *see if they need volunteers*
4) *spend all free time at that boarding school*
5) *keep silent until the world makes sense again*

Right now, she didn't know when that would be.

From a distance, Jett watched the chaos at her home disperse as the uniformed intruders and their equipment left. Daddio restrained Mother, who seemed angry that Jett was on Ben's porch. After one last pointed look, Mother stomped back into the house. Good. Jett's resolve to stay in front of Ben's door until he opened it remained unchallenged.

Daddio sat on the bench outside their door, watching and waiting for her to give up. Jett hoped he was prepared for a good long wait. She wanted to know what happened.

She wanted Yoda. She wanted Ben. She wanted life as it had been.

But it wasn't and it wouldn't be ever again. She looked toward her home. Daddio was still there, sitting on the front porch. He waited and she knew he would be there when she was ready to go home. Or when she wasn't, but came home anyway. He would be there. And Yoda would still be gone.

18

OVER THE NEXT two weeks, the air around her home turned stormy and volatile. It choked her. And each day, it was getting worse. Jett burrowed further into the nest of blankets.

Her parents were fighting. Again. She didn't even need to *try* to listen. The argument invaded her space, her world. She couldn't get away. She pulled the pile of quilts closer onto her body and hid as much as she could. She wanted it all to just go away.

"Kathy, just give her some time. She's thinking. Jett's analyzing something, and we need to just let her be."

"Are you serious? Really? It's been 12 days. *Twelve days!* Our daughter went *missing!* For *hours!* We don't know where she went, what happened, or who she encountered. At the *very* least, I think she needs a full evaluation, both physical and mental. What if she was raped? She's not speaking and there's got to be a reason. I promise you.

There's. A. Reason! Either someone did something to her or she's done something. This is a reaction. Can't you see? She's being willfully defiant in a way she hasn't been before. I don't know what's happened, but what I do know is that we need to get her to a hospital. Doctors. Professionals. Specialists. *Now!* It may already be too late." Her mother spoke with a desperate passion that Jett didn't recognize, like she was pleading for a life.

This confused her.

"What are you *talking* about, too late? She is here. She's home. She's safe. She hasn't even *tried* to leave. She'll be fine. She's sleeping. That's what teenagers do! So what if she isn't talking? Not everyone wants to talk about everything. If she doesn't want to talk, that's fine. Do you blame her? Look at how we're speaking to each other. Would you speak up, if you were her?"

The floorboards stopped creaking and the house went silent. Jett focused on releasing tension by rhythmically moving her fingers against her palms. Then Daddio tried a different tactic.

"Yeah, I guess *you* would, but you know what? *I* wouldn't. I'd be in my room playing a video game. I'd be sneaking all the treats upstairs with me. I'd be reading a book or watching a movie. I'd be shutting out the old people yelling at each other. I'd be *escaping*. We're not taking her to your colleague Amy or any other kind of doctor. And that is *final!*"

Daddio rarely put his foot down, rarely vetoed Mother's ideas. But this time he was adamant, and that made Mother pause. Both were silent for a moment but it was a different kind of silence. For a moment, Jett could breathe.

Mother's voice cut back in, but this time it was small, broken. "I'm worried, Joe. I'm really, really worried. What if she starts hurting herself? We're right here and we wouldn't even know. She won't even look at me. She just holds up a hand and turns away. What the hell did I do? How could she treat me this way?"

Jett was surprised that Mother didn't understand. Wasn't it obvious? She let complete strangers into their home and gave them access to Jett's work. She was treating her mother exactly how Mother treated her when she couldn't be bothered to explain something. Why was this baffling to her?

It sounded like Daddio moved closer; his voice dropped a few decibels. "But if she *were* hurt? We would know. Seriously, I believe we would know. One of us is always invading her privacy, always right there. She literally has no privacy. None. We took the doors off her bedroom *and* the bathrooms. She literally cannot shut us out. For goodness' sake, every night, one of us sleeps on a makeshift bed in the hallway. All she has is her silence. Give her that. Give her time. Please."

Jett didn't hear any more. Her eyelids were heavy. She couldn't stay awake a moment longer. She knew she was processing a lot, even if she didn't understand exactly what just yet. She knew her body needed sleep. She couldn't get up. She couldn't speak. She couldn't alleviate their fears, even if she tried. Giving in, she went back to sleep.

Jett woke up to more of these conversations, this time in low, muted tones. At one point she heard a voice that wasn't her parents. It sounded like it might even be Ben. But that didn't make sense. Wasn't Mother pushing for doctors and specialists? For Amy? No, it couldn't be Ben. Mother had been mean to her one local friend. She stayed in her nest but angled closer to the door. She wanted to hear this.

"Ma'am, sir, I know we got off on the wrong foot. I apologize for any part I may have played in that. I also apologize for not introducing myself sooner, but I'm here now. My name is Benjamin Calbert-Otto. I am 36 years old. I live alone, but I do own my property.

"This year, I decided to volunteer as a puppy parent for Bergin University of Canine Studies. The pup was three months old when he came to me. Jett and I became friends through my pup—our pup, really. She named him Yoda. I'm missing him terribly now that he's back at boarding school and I think Jett might be as well.

"Would it be all right if I gave her the gift I brought for her? I wasn't sure which holiday traditions you honor, so I specifically brought it over after all the holidays were celebrated. Please let me see her."

Jett's heart fluttered. It *was* Ben. Would she really get to see him today? This was such an unexpected treat. She leaned closer, waiting for them to accept. She crossed her fingers. In her head, she begged Daddio to say "yes."

What did this long silence mean? She held her breath. Would they let her see Ben? She certainly hoped so. She certainly wanted to. So, although no one saw, Jett nodded.

Daddio answered. She thought that was a good sign.

"Ben, thank you for your bravery. It took guts to approach us after the way you were treated and I, for one, am sorry for the way it was handled. My name is Joe and this is my wife Kathy. We were unaware she had made a friend in the neighborhood. She never even told us about Yoda. You say she was very attached, but this is all new information to me, to us. And I'm uncomfortable allowing you access to our daughter unmonitored until I run a background check. You do understand, don't you?"

"I'm trying to. Really, I am. Can I see her with supervision?"

Evidently, Mother was not pacified. "Ben, I don't know who you think you are, but I'm her mother and she won't even see me. I'm not certain she'll want to see you and even if she did, she won't say anything. She's not talking. So, what do you want me to do?"

"Kathy, ma'am, I don't know what's going on with you and Jett, and I don't know why she won't talk to you, but maybe you can text her to ask whether she'll see me. I have a feeling this gift might cheer her up."

After a few moments of weighted silence, Jett felt her phone vibrate with a text from Daddio.

> Sweetie, Ben is here. He wants to see you. Do you want to see him? Will you come down? I can take him into the study...

Her eyes widened and she touched her throat. Ben was so smart. She could text! She should have thought of that sooner.

Immediately she fired off her reply.

> Daddio, tell Ben this, exactly: I WANT TO SEE MY CHUM, EVEN WHEN I AM GLUM. And Daddio? You can come too, but not Mom. She's still mean to him. I'll meet you in the study in a few minutes. xo

She heard the chime of Daddio's phone. He must have read it. "Kathy, I need you to pick up the dinner we ordered. It's at that place in Strawberry where we usually get dim sum."

Mother huffed. "Okay, but first, what did Jett say? Will she talk to him?"

"Um, no. She didn't say she would talk to him. I just got a text that our order is about ready and you know Jett doesn't like reheated Chinese food. Aren't you hungry? In the meanwhile, I'll show Ben out."

She heard Mother grab her keys. She heard the garage door open. She thought she heard murmured words between Ben and Daddio. As the voices grew quieter, she knew they were headed to the study, not the front door. Jett got up, stretched, and ran her fingers through her hair. She went to her bathroom, gargled mouthwash, then eagerly crept downstairs and went directly to the study.

She waved at the two of them as she entered, giving a thumbs up to Daddio for the clever way he had redirected Mother. Then she turned all attention to her brave and loyal visitor. She rocked on her heels, hands clasped behind her back, smiling broadly. Did he have any idea how glad she was to see him? Oh, how she wanted to tell him, to speak the words and make sure that he knew. She opened her mouth, but no sound came out. Jett swallowed, blew out a breath and tried again. Still, no words. She frowned, shook her head and tried one more time. When did she lose the choice to speak? Both of them were watching her struggle and that made it so much worse.

Quietly, Ben gave her a verbal boost. "Oh, chum, you are so very *glum*! Your father showed me your message as we waited. I had no idea this was eating you alive. How will you survive?"

Moved by how sweet he was being, even after dealing with her mean mother, Jett tried opening her mouth again to speak, but no sound came out. She looked for her phone. Dang. She must have left it upstairs. Desperate, she looked for a notecard or a piece of paper—anything!—so she could tell Ben what she wanted him to know. But it was overwhelming. This inability to speak and her conflicting desire to talk was overwhelming. Jett could feel her body overloading and starting to shut down again. She fought it.

She had expected she could go back to speaking whenever she wanted. But maybe this silence wasn't so voluntary or in her control. Feeling the mounting evidence of her "not normal," a single tear rolled down her cheek. She looked at Ben, wanting him to see, wanting him to know—everything.

"Oh, Jett! Oh, Jett. How your silence is making me fret. It's painful to see you this upset."

He held out the carefully wrapped package he had brought her.

As she took it, Jett stared in wonder. Gold ribbon hugged thick white paper. She looked for tape but didn't see any and the seams were almost invisible. Did Ben do that or was it wrapped by a professional? She couldn't decide whether to open it or leave it as it was so she could admire it a little longer.

Ben saw Jett's work covering one of the walls like a piece of abstract art. "Your work! Jett, I see! You've done so much! It fills me with glee. May I take a closer look? Study it more? You know I can't help it. I've never seen this before."

Jett nodded sadly, thinking of the thieves who, with Mother's permission, had stolen her intellectual property. She thought how outraged Ben would be if he knew all her work had been pilfered. She motioned for him to look, even as she decided to take it down as soon as he left. It didn't matter now anyway.

With his hands clasped behind his back respectfully, Ben studied her findings. She moved to stand beside him.

"You are remarkable, Jett, truly exceptional." He pointed to the lines she had placed tying ideas together. "This is art. Thank you for allowing me to witness how your genius works." He gestured at the package in her hands. "Will you open your gift? It's after Hanukkah and Christmas so we're not breaking any rules if you open it now."

Jett smiled tentatively as she carefully unwrapped it. Nestled inside an ornately decorated box, layers of tissue paper protected a framed picture of Yoda. She remembered that moment. On the trail leading into Tiburon, Yoda had been acting up. Jett stopped their walk and tried various hand signals to see if he picked up her queues. He had. And, this moment? It happened just after she praised his attentiveness. Yoda was grinning a full smile, tongue lolling, but sitting confidently, staring at her. Ben must've taken the picture from just behind her because she hadn't seen it before. Jett hugged it to her heart tightly as her eyes overflowed.

"Doodlebug," her father said softly. "You're squeezing awfully tight. Be sure you don't break it. I want to see when you're ready to share."

She bounded over to him, her smile beaming through her tears as she showed him the picture. Just then, she heard the garage door open.

"Well, that's my cue," Ben said. "Joe, thank you for facilitating our time. I'm just going to sneak out the front. Jett, I don't want to go so long without seeing you, even without Yoda. Let me know if you want help with your project. You've really got something good going there."

Jett waved with her free hand, the framed picture of Yoda still firmly held to her chest. She hoped he could see the gratitude she could not say.

As Daddio followed him out of the room, she turned to look at the work. Her shoulders slumped. Too bad it was compromised. What was she going to do now? Jett looked at the picture of Yoda. If that wonderful puppy could do hard things, so could she.

Carefully, she set down the picture and walked to the wall. After admiring it for a moment, she took a shuddering breath and began to dismantle all she had gathered about teenagers worth watching. The Breakfast Club Sorting

System was the first thing to come down. Lastly, she removed all the clues to this thing called love. She put that material into a box she found under the desk. She needed to pass it on to her Core5 in case they could still use it. Soon they would become the Core4.

After all, how could she participate if she couldn't communicate? Jett was done with love. Someone else would just have to figure it out.

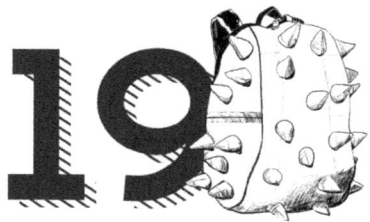

A FEW DAYS later, Jett listened to the low tones of another urgent "conversation" in which, as usual, her parental units were not agreeing.

They were just out of view and it was Mother's turn to volley. "I hear you, Joe. I see your point. And I *don't* want to make life any more stressful for our daughter."

"Stop managing me, Kath. Just stop already."

"Okay, but I also don't see it that way. Let me just finish."

Jett felt the tension in their silence. She tiptoed quietly so she could peek down the stairs. Would they catch her watching? Floorboards creaked. Someone must be pacing. Yep. She knew that footfall. Daddio. He must have given Mother the go-ahead to keep talking.

"I see her going to school today as a way to reclaim her usual routine. Jett likes school. She may actually decide to speak there. Besides, everyone else is returning from winter break so it won't seem odd for her to show up, too. It would be odder if she didn't. Starting back up today is normal. If she's a bit quieter than usual, I bet you no one will even notice. Besides, it's time we stopped alternating schedules for the 24/7 watch. It's time we went back to our own routines, to our lives."

When Jett heard this, she sighed in relief. Finally.

"*Really*? Get back to our *routines*? Get back to *our lives*? At the risk of Jett losing hers?"

She could hear incredulity dripping from his words.

"You're the one who convinced me something may be seriously wrong. Now you're changing your tune? We haven't even reinstalled the doors we took down—at your insistence, I might add! Do you remember telling me we had to watch her every moment? And now, out of the blue, you want to just go back to our *lives*?" His volume was beginning to crescendo.

Jett guessed his skin was a mottled red. She could hear the frustration as he paced.

"At what cost? What are you willing to sacrifice for your precious 'life'? Our daughter?"

Is this what sneering sounded like? His words were redolent of disgust and emotional exhaustion. This was the tone Daddio usually reserved for real trauma. Were they in trauma? Was that why the doors were off? She had wondered about that.

"Joe, thank you for taking my concerns seriously, but I'm at my wit's end. I can't do this anymore. It's been three weeks! I promise I won't just send her to school. I'll consult with the administration first. You know, they do have a counselor of some sort on staff. I've heard he's quite good. Will that help? Don't you have back-to-back client meetings and court today? You go. I'll deal with this and let you know the resolution."

She could hear Daddio muttering something, but Mother insisted. "I'll stay home again if that's what's needed, but I just don't think it is anymore."

Heavy footsteps followed a beat of silence. The door from the kitchen into the garage slammed. Jett heard the garage door open and then the sound of his car pulling out of the driveway as it closed again.

She wished she could talk to her dad, even call out to him before he left. But she remained trapped in her silence. All this drama was so tiring and now Daddio had left for work without even a goodbye. As she curled into herself at the top of the stairs, Jett faded out.

Mother's professional voice brought her back into focus. She must be on the phone. "Yes. Thank you. Mr. Williams? Hello, this is Katherine Harper, Jett's mother. Do you have a moment? Oh, good. Yes, it's nice to meet you, too."

Why was she calling Mr. Williams? Jett hoped he didn't mention her having to redo the first paper. She wanted to creep closer to listen, but her eyelids were too heavy to keep open. She crept back into her room, to her cozy warm bed, for a quick nap.

Abruptly, Jett woke to find her mother standing over her, with crossed arms and her face screwed up tight, observing as she slept. This expression was nuanced in Mother's nonverbal vocabulary; Jett didn't presume to know what it meant right now. Trying to maintain a neutral expression, she blinked at her and waited for an explanation.

"Hey, Jett. I know it's super early, but you have an appointment with Mr. Williams before class this morning. I made you a lunch and I bet your bag for school is already packed. Can you be ready to go in five minutes? I'm gonna go wait in my car."

Jett stretched like a cat waking from a nap. She moved slowly, but nodded. She already was ready and wanted to hand off the Foundations project to her former team. They would need her work, in whatever state it was in, now that she would be leaving Presidio Prep. They needed to finish it before the thieves from the other night used it for their own gain.

Jett was curious. How did communication with Mr. Williams—with anyone, really—work without using your vocal cords? And how quickly would they want her gone? Would she at least get a chance to see her team? Memorize them before leaving?

Her eyes started to sting but Jett sucked back the tears and swallowed hard. Would they send her to boarding school or would Mother homeschool her? And if so, how exactly would *that* work?

Mother called out. "Jett?"

Go time. Jett picked up her stuff and started out the door. She squared her shoulders to face the day. Ready or not, it was time.

———>◆<———

CARLOS CAUGHT UP to her as she walked across the field toward the main building. He seemed excited.

"Hey, 'Manita! ¡Feliz navidad y prospero año nuevo! I have something for you. I'll bring it to class. Are you excited about the new year?"

She stared at him. Jett would miss this crazy boy who may or may not be brain damaged. She still wasn't convinced he was right in the head. Jett looked down at the box in her hands. He'd said he had something for her. Should she have brought something else for her team—besides months of research and all her carefully documented notes? Wait—was he talking about presents? Although all of the holidays were over, that thought hadn't occurred to her. Oh, well. Her work was the best gift she could give anyway. Jett handed it to him.

"Oh! For me? Sweet! I'll take it now but open it in class. Looks like you didn't wrap either. Ha! My Mamá insisted I wrap the regalos. I'll try not to peek. I've got to go finish up a practice. See you soon, eh?" Carlos leaned in, kissed her cheek, and rushed off.

She was stunned. Jett wasn't used to easy affection from anyone. And yet from Carlos it was only shocking in how easy it was to accept. Was that because she loved him? Did he love her? Sighing and continuing toward the main building, Jett put a hand to her cheek to press it in. It didn't matter now. She would be done with all of this soon. Memories would be all she had. Jett closed her eyes to seal in the moment.

She wondered what she would do after she no longer was part of the Presidio Prep student body. Where would she go?

She saw Mr. Williams on the front porch of the administration building and her steps slowed under the weight of all she was about to lose. He lifted a hand in welcome as she approached. Well, here goes everything, she thought, nodding a greeting as she reached him.

"There you are, Jett! I'm glad you made it. Let's go inside where I can run my mouth without interruption, shall we?" Mr. Williams grinned and wiggled his eyebrows at her.

Was he really so happy to be dismissing her? At least he was doing so in private. If only she could say 'thank you' to him for his part in her life. Suddenly her eyes welled up. She was crying and she couldn›t even explain why. Jett thought about it. Huh. Maybe this, too, was love. She was going to miss him.

They walked in together and Mr. Williams closed the door to his office behind her before he saw the tears running down her face. He looked shocked.

"Oh, Jett. Hey, there." He ducked his head and approached her carefully with a box of tissues, peering into her face, lowering his voice soothingly. "Hey, there. Hey-hey."

He breathed deeply. "Okay. Let's take a moment and breathe together." They did.

"Yes. Like that. Again."

And they did again. When her system calmed down enough to breathe steadily without direction, they stood in silence. Jett looked up at Mr. Williams. He motioned for her to take a seat before bringing a chair around to sit next to her, both of them looking out over his desk and through his picture window to the bay far below.

"Your Mom called. She's ... she's a 'wow.'"

Jett rolled her eyes; she couldn't agree more. She wondered whether he'd caught her eye roll with his peripheral vision. Whether he had or not, Jett liked sitting side-by-side like this. It felt less intense, less demanding not to be expected to maintain eye contact.

"I'll leave it at that," he said. "I know I've got the added pressure of all the words for us today, but that doesn't mean I'm not expecting you to find a way to tell me things. Do you know any ASL? American Sign Language? This is 'yes.'" He made a fist and waved it up and down. "This is 'no.'" He did a funny-looking finger gesture that reminded Jett of birds peeping.

Jett was surprised by all the things he seemed to know.

"We can use those and play '20 Questions.' But when you're in class, you're gonna have to type into the notes app on your phone and show it to whomever you want to know something. Okay? Let's practice."

Jett signed 'yes.' But she was confused. He said 'when she was in class.' Wasn't she being kicked out? Suspended, at the very least? She pulled out her phone to ask but he put up a hand.

"I want to start with our game, okay? You can type to me afterward." Mr. Williams waited for her to agree. Instead, she tried that sign that looked like a talking bird that meant 'no.' To her surprise, he smiled. Maybe he should sit behind his desk again. She wasn't sure she could do this side-by-side after all. It was less pressure, but was she understanding less because she couldn't read his body language as well? She didn't know and she needed clarity. Quickly, she typed out a note.

"I don't understand. I thought I was here to be released. Isn't this an exit interview? Are you telling me I am not being asked to leave? Am I being put on suspension?"

Mr. Williams read it and reared back in his chair. He turned to look directly at her. "Jett! Is that what you thought? Who told you that? How did you come to that..."

He stopped, pinching the bridge of his nose. After a moment, he tried again.

"Well, then, before we play our game, let me just state this for the record. We need you. You're not being invited to leave or go anywhere *but* here." He turned his chair to look her fully in the face, just inches away, fierce loyalty bleeding into his tone.

"We need Jett Harper, as she is, with or without speech. I am *not* letting you disappear on me. You got that? *That* is not an option."

Her tears started again.

Mr. Williams stood up.

"Okay, Jett. I apologize," he said, handing her the box of tissues before walking around his desk. "I thought sitting next to you would make this easier but maybe that only works when you are verbal. I'm going to give you some space so we can try this again, okay?"

Did he understand her tears were born of relief mingled with confusion? How would this work, exactly, if she couldn't talk? There was so much she wanted to ask, but couldn't. For example, she knew speaking was expected. Not speaking? Well, that just wasn't normal, was it? She didn't know anyone who couldn't speak. She looked down at her hands as she thought this through. Silence may not be normal for her old life, but it was for her, for right now. She looked up and nodded for him to continue, signing: "Yes. *Yes*. YES!" She wanted to know more.

"Okay, Jett. Forget games. Let's just try to have a conversation. Me talking and you sorting out how to communicate while not using your voice. This is doable. We're gonna sort out 'the how.'"

For the next 25 minutes, they worked on communicating. Jett watched his hunched shoulders ease downward as her body relaxed. She could do this. She wanted to speak so badly. She felt like it was almost possible—"almost" being the operative word. Intermittently, she tried talking and failed. Maybe it would happen again. One day. Soon? Who knew? Whenever it was, that would have to be soon enough.

"I already told your teachers you're not to speak out loud, but I want to know, who are your friends? Who will notice your vow of silence?"

Jett shook her head and signed no, simultaneously. Did she have any friends? Really? Had she heard anyone use that term to describe *her*? Not that she could remember. Who would notice? No one would notice, except maybe her teammates. And when they did, this wasn't going to work. She was a freak, a crazy, broken freak. Deaf people and mute people weren't. But they didn't speak one day and then not the next.

He continued. "Hmph. Okay then. Tell me who is in your Core5?"

Jett listed their names on her notes app. He looked it over, making noises to himself; she wondered if he knew how much that revealed. Finally, Mr. Williams looked at his watch and picked up his phone.

"Yes, good morning, Ms. Diaz. Nice to speak with you again. Just wanted to remind you, Jett's taken a vow of silence. She and I are working on a special project," he said, winking broadly at her.

"Don't let anyone give her a hard time. If someone does, I want to know about it. Oh, and when you see Sam from her Core5, please ask her to come see me. Thanks, and yes, speak soon." Mr. Williams hung up and propped his elbows on his desk, interlacing his fingers.

Jett thought staying at Presidio Prep was the best surprise. But—now what? She couldn't speak, she didn't know sign language, and she didn't have an interpreter. How was this going to work? Jett couldn't quite wrap her mind around it.

Speaking of wrapping—now that she knew she was staying, Jett wondered what gifts to get her Core5. She would have to shop online as soon as possible. Maybe she could do it at lunch and pick things up after school. Except, how was she going to communicate *that*? Jett bet the gifts could just be delivered to her home or Daddio's office. That would be easier than picking them up. Oh! Also, who in her home ever did any gift wrapping? She laughed to herself trying to imagine Daddio with paper, tape, scissors, and ribbon. No, Mother usually did the gift wrapping and would do it for her, if asked. The thought of

Jett giving gifts to her friends might make Mother happy. She would have to text her parents to keep them updated, but that could wait a bit. Worry weighed down tentative hope and excitement. Her body felt heavy. Soon everyone would know for sure that she wasn't normal.

Sam walked in. She didn't knock and the closed door didn't slow her. She just walked right in. This shocked Jett. Was this normal? It had never occurred to her to do such a thing. Heart speeding up with nerves and anticipation, Jett watched as Sam walked up to the desk.

"Hi, Mr. Williams, I'm Sam Walker. Oh, hey, Jett." Sam smiled at her before turning back to Mr. Williams. "I hear you asked to see me?"

"Hi, Sam. Nice to meet you. I did. I have a special project for you. It involves Jett. Are you up for it?"

Sam folded her arms and squinted her eyes, but nodded her assent.

"Good. Okay, then. Your teammate Jett is on a break from talking. She is not using her voice. At all. I need you to be her voice. Can you do that?"

Sam looked startled as she absorbed this odd request.

"What? Jett's like—mute? For how long? Does this mean we can have phone privileges in class? That would be cool!" Sam was warming up to the idea. She looked at Jett. "I need your number and you need mine."

"Actually," Mr. Williams said, smiling, "I'm granting phone privileges to your whole team as long as someone sticks by her side all day and acts as her voice. I don't know for how long yet." He looked at Jett and paused for a moment, then focused back on Sam. "We're still working that out. Are you in?"

"Definitely, I'm in. Can't speak for anyone else, but I am." She shrugged as she turned to Jett. "I don't get it, but hey, girlfriend! You found a way that we get to use our phones in *class!* Thanks!"

Jett felt relief washing over her. She was pleased, but embarrassed by all the attention, and hoped Sam would stay on her side. She wanted to act like it was no big deal, so she shrugged, too. She couldn't believe how Mr. Williams was treating this huge thing. Because of him, it almost seemed like no big deal, a game even. She appreciated how easily he accepted this—this whatever it was. It was uncomfortable and decidedly *not* fun. She hated not being able to choose to use her voice. She hated that her body wasn't obeying her. But somehow Mr. Williams had made this okay. Jett was grateful.

Gathering her things, she stood up to go with Sam. Jett turned and lifted her fingers in her usual farewell to Mr. Williams; he returned the gesture.

"One more thing," he said as they started to leave. "I'm assuming no one else on the team knows this yet, so it's up to you to get it across, Sam. Can you do that?" He looked for her confirmation. "Okay, then. Thank you for your help."

Once they were outside, Sam put a hand on Jett's arm to draw her aside. "Jett, is it true? You can't speak or you won't speak?"

Jett shook her head. She wasn't sure when it had changed, but it had started out as a choice, but now it wasn't. For now, she was firmly in the camp of "couldn't."

"Well, I'm not sure what this is, but you can tell me if you want. I'm not gonna judge. I owe you one, for my music. And I keep secrets too. You can totally trust me. But if not? No biggie. We all have things we can't or won't share."

They kept walking towards class. But Sam stopped her again.

"Hey! I just thought of something. You seemed pretty stressed about me knowing you've got this silent thing going on. And we all know Carlos and Ruby are not the most —" She struggled for a word. "Ummm—understanding ones. They might give you a hard time, ya know. Ruby for sure is gonna nag you." She frowned at this thought. "Do you want the others in our Core5 to know? I mean, if we can keep it down to you, me, and Andy, would that work? I think that would work better."

Jett nodded enthusiastically. That would totally work. She saw Sam's wisdom.

"Yeah. Okay, so our Core5 just became Inner3. Let me text Andy." She pulled out her phone and thumb-typed a message. Instantly, he replied.

"He's in. We can do this." Sam nudged Jett with her shoulder, and Jett was pleased to see warmth in her eyes. Was this love?

Just before they entered the classroom, Sam stopped her one more time. "Want to hang out with me and get into some music later?"

Jett, realizing the implications of this, beamed a smile of understanding at Sam. She was her friend in class and, soon, outside of class, too.

Jett could hardly believe it. What a day!

20

WHEN SHE AND Sam entered their Foundations Class, small groups dotted the classroom landscape. Each team huddled in their own secret meeting. It looked to Jett like they were all super-absorbed in their own projects, in their own worlds. Good!

Jett looked around with fresh appreciation, grateful she was still here. Her eyes landed on Ruby and Andy, sitting in their usual spot. Ruby was on her phone, as usual, getting in the last few digital moments before it had to be put away. How would she react to Sam, Andy, and Jett having phone privileges when she, Ruby, did not? How long could they hide their privilege? Why should they? After all, Ms. Diaz knew. She expected the whole group to be using their phones, but only her group. Jett knew Sam looked forward to *not* letting Ruby and Carlos use theirs, since they weren't part of the Inner3. They were not on the trusted and helpful list. Should she tell Mr. Williams? She wondered how he would react.

Jett checked out Andy's socks. Did he get new ones for the holidays? What did his family celebrate? Were presents a part of their culture, too? Today Andy wore navy blue socks with red buckets of popcorn, spilled popcorn pieces all over them. These may be her favorite yet. Movie popcorn socks! Who knew? Jett wondered if she could find him even better ones. She put socks on her phone next to his name and started to consider what to get the rest of her Core5.

As Jett watched her, Ruby looked up from her phone. Their eyes met and Ruby quickly looked back down. Jett wondered what Ruby could possibly want for a gift. She knew from the media hype that Ruby really did have everything. Hmmm. She was a hard one. Jett thought back to the day she had left Ruby with those human vipers. Maybe what Ruby needed was a reminder she had real friends. Jett decided to get her one of those word affirmation bracelets that she saw others wearing. She could buy her a cool friendship bracelet and simply write: "Because we are" on the note. Yeah! That would work. Would it make it true? She hoped so. Jett smiled as she added that to her gifts list.

She moved on to Sam. She was easy: Sam loved music. She also knew Daddio had connections to get her into really cool concerts at the Fillmore. Now she just needed to sort out what was coming up for her and Sam to go to.

That left Carlos, who at that exact moment—just after she wrote "music" next to Sam on her list—came running into class, arms stretched around an overflow of presents.

"Hola! Hi! I'm here! I'm here. Sorry, I'm a little late. I can't wait for us all to exchange gifts! Here, Linda, you first." He handed the top package to Ruby and set the rest on his desk before putting his hands on his hips. He watched everyone's faces as they looked at his bounty. "Well, where's mine? I mean, I know we didn't say anything, but we *are* going to exchange gifts today, right?" Carlos vibrated with excitement as the group looked around at each other.

Sam started laughing. Jett's eyebrows rose. Andy looked sheepish and Ruby sighed. She answered first. "Carlos, you dolt. We didn't decide we would give each other gifts *at all*. And if I had one for you, I didn't plan for us to exchange in class today!" She rolled her eyes heavenward as if Carlos were the dramatic one.

"But Linda! Seriously? Jett already gave me mine. I told her I would wait to open it. It was hard, especially since it isn't wrapped, but I've been waiting!" His last words kind of sounded like a whine to Jett and she covered her mouth with her hands so he wouldn't see her reaction. Carlos held up the box she had given him that morning in triumph, like it was a true prize.

Sam looked to Jett, who just shook her head no, trying to tell Sam that it wasn't a gift but Sam went on the attack before getting Jett's meaning.

"Carlos, you perv! Did you take Jett's box? Gimme that!" Sam snatched the box and plunked it down in front of Jett before anyone else could move.

Carlos looked like he might cry, snatch it back, or fight. He turned to Jett, who looked down, unable to meet his gaze. This was all her fault. She pushed her phone to Sam, notes app opened.

"Ask them if we can exchange gifts tomorrow."

Sam read the note and shook her head.

Opening her eyes extra wide, Jett pinned Sam with an intense stare and frowned. Sam wouldn't stop shaking her head.

Jett didn't give up. She passed Sam a new note. "ASK THEM. Whatever your hang up, we can talk about it later."

Sam looked at the final note, glanced at Jett, then back down at the note before sighing in defeat.

The group watched and waited to be let in on what was going on. Even Ruby was paying attention.

Jett raised her chin and looked back at them defiantly. She could do this. Mr. Williams said she could, and Sam said she and Andy would help. Now was Sam's chance to prove it. Jett laced her fingers together, just as she had seen Mr. Williams do earlier this morning, and she stared into Sam.

"All right. All right!" Sam huffed and turned her attention to the group. "Can we just exchange gifts in our group tomorrow? Sounds like Ruby, Jett, and I all need time to prepare." She turned to Andy. "Andy, what about you? Wanna get your gifts on tomorrow?"

Andy still looked sheepish but shrugged his assent. He peeked at Jett. Now everyone was looking at Jett, especially Carlos, who looked baffled and dejected.

"'Manita, what happened?" he said in a tiny voice. "I told you I don't care if it's wrapped. I can wait until tomorrow, but please can I have it back?"

Jett focused on the box in her hands, wishing she could shrink smaller and smaller, wishing she could fit into the box.

"Please, 'Manita. I will love it. I will! Just give it back and tell me what's going on."

A single tear slid down her cheek. She wanted to explain. Jett hated how quickly miscommunication happened without words. She used to believe language was the main culprit in misunderstandings. Now she realized how precious a common language could be. Language wasn't so awful. Not being able to speak was. Especially when you were used to blurting out whatever came to mind. That was awful.

Insistent feelings and unexpressed thoughts weighed her down. They leaked from her eyes. Jett tucked her chin into her chest, hoping no one saw. But they all did.

"Whoa, girl. Pull it together," Ruby commanded. "It's an ugly box but he wants it. Just give it to him. Seriously. I don't think he'll even care what horrible thing you found for him."

But that was it, wasn't it? Jett hadn't found anything for Carlos. She hadn't even pieced together what she *would* find for him. And by tomorrow?

As Ruby tried to comfort her, Jett didn't know which was worse, the miscommunication or Ruby showing her sympathy. Was Ruby's caring even real? More tears fell and her eyelids grew heavy. She was overloading fast and just wanted to take a nap. Jett rested her head on the offensive box that started it all.

Andy nudged Sam, who shrugged. Carlos looked ready to cry and Ruby threw her hands up in the air. "You," she said, pointing at Andy. "What's your name? Come with me." Andy followed her as Ruby marched up to the front of the classroom.

"Ms. Diaz, we have a problem. Jett's a mess. I think someone broke her. It's bad and I can't deal with her drama. Someone needs to fix this."

Ms. Diaz looked from Ruby to Andy to Jett and back to the two students standing in front of her. Ruby had her arms crossed. Andy was standing awkwardly next to her. "Okay, team. What do you propose we do?"

"*Fix* her," Ruby demanded. "Send her to that counselor guy, or whatever, but get her out of here and *fix* her."

Jett wanted nothing more than for a hole to open up in the classroom and swallow her. "Andy, you take over," Ms. Diaz said as Andy grimaced and nodded. "Would you mind taking Jett to see Dr. Williams? I believe they have a special project they are working on, anyway. Ruby, you can hand me your phone. You won't be needing it for *at least* the rest of the class."

Ruby looked stunned. "Doctor? Did you just say 'doctor'? Isn't that a bit of an overreaction to someone being a freak?"

"Really? Okay, that's it," Ms. Diaz seethed. "The world is gonna thank me. Ruby, I'm going to keep your phone for the entire day and put you on warning. Don't try me. I know you think your opinion is all that matters, but I assure you, it doesn't matter at all. The sooner you learn that, the sooner this world will be a better place. Andy, take Jett to Dr. Williams' office now, please."

Ruby huffed as crimson bloomed up her neck and onto her cheeks. Andy smiled a small, private smile and walked back to Jett, who remained motionless, looking off into space and on the verge of falling asleep.

Gently touching her shoulder, he urged her to stand. "Jett? We've got to go. You and me. I can carry Carlos' present. Take your cool spiky pack and let's, you know—go?"

Jett looked up into his pleading expression and nodded once. She didn't know why, but she would go with him. As they left the class, Jett overheard Carlos wail, "'MA-NI-TA!"

She looked back, but Andy took her hand, coaxing her along, just like her dad did when Mother insisted they get moving.

"What has happened to my 'Manita? Sam, tell me everything! Why does Andy have my gift? This isn't *normal*!"

Jett wanted to turn around. She wanted to reassure him, tell him everything. Poor Carlos. How was she going to help her friend? She wanted to make it all right. She just didn't know how. The stress made her so tired. Jett really wished her voice would start working again.

21

WALKING WITH ANDY to Mr. Williams' office, Jett couldn't shake the sound of Carlos's pain. Her heart was sinking. She fretted over her inability to resolve his confusion. She fretted over his plaintive cry that this wasn't normal. Was her fate sealed? Would she never be normal?

Each of the three people who spent enough time with her to have an opinion on the matter saw abnormalities in her: Mother, Mr. Williams, and now Carlos. But it also seemed as if they each meant something different when they said she was "not normal." Hearing it certainly felt different from each of them. Were definitions so fluid? She'd have to think about that later.

Meanwhile, Jett just wanted to celebrate. Sam *had* asked her to hang out, basically confirming they were friends outside of class *and* in. Did that make her Jett's first everywhere friend? No. No, that would have to be Carlos, although she hadn't thought of him that way before. Plus, time with Sam in public, outside of class, hadn't happened yet—but it would. That would make Sam her second everywhere friend, right? Unless this walk with Andy counted as friends outside of class. Would Andy count it that way? Jett wasn't sure. He had been told to take her. So maybe he was just doing his duty and Sam would be her second everywhere friend. She wanted to ask someone about all of this, but she had no voice to do so and it was too much to type. Besides, her head already hurt from trying to sort it all out. Oh, how she wanted to just crawl off in a corner somewhere and sleep.

Jett's reverie was interrupted as they entered Mr. Williams' office. She paid close attention as Andy announced them.

"Mr. Williams? Or should I call you 'Doctor?'"

"Most students call me Mr. Williams and that's fine by me. While it's true I went to medical school and then went on to specialize in psychiatry, I decided to work here because keeping up with college-bound leaders like you sounded like fun. You lot certainly keep me on my toes!"

Andy dipped his head in acknowledgement. Clearly, this made sense to *him*. "Okay, then. Well." He shoved his hands into the front pockets of his jeans.

Jett wondered if he was nervous. She hadn't seen this mannerism from him before.

"I've been given the honor of bringing Jett to you. She's not speaking and our teacher says you'll know what to do. Is this true? Do you know what to do? Can you bring Jett back to us?"

When it became clear that Mr. Williams wasn't going to tell him anything until he knew more about what had happened, Andy haltingly went on.

"Something happened, I think. Ruby said someone broke her. Is *that* true? I'm taking martial arts. Do you need me to defend her? Guard her? Shadow her? If someone hurt her, I'm not okay with that. You know, I'm in most of her classes and I can switch to the one we don't share. Or, maybe Sam can take over for that class. She seems pretty tough."

Mr. Williams held up one finger to get Andy to pause and then addressed Jett. "It's clear you've got a loyal fan here, but it looks like you need a break. Do you want to hang out here with me for a bit?"

With her focus fading in and out, Jett struggled to respond. Eventually, though, she shrugged. Her head lolled as her vision blurred. Looking up through heavy eyelids, she thought Mr. Williams looked confused. What confused him? Her listlessness or Andy's clear hesitation to leave her side? Andy's subtle but firm fighting stance told her he was ready for defense. He looked strong and Jett wasn't sure how much longer she could stand there. She leaned against him.

"To answer your questions: I have no answers—yet. But I will. Don't worry. The rest of your Core5 must be concerned, too. Will you please go back to class and assure everyone that Jett is exactly as she should be? Tell them I'm not worried. Tell them I promise to share more when I know more—*if* it's mine to tell."

Mr. Williams moved from behind his desk and shook Andy's hand, putting his other hand on Andy's shoulder and turning him toward the door.

Jett swayed as her pillar shifted. Mr. Williams reached out. He held her elbow to steady her. When she stopped swaying, he dropped his hold.

"Thanks, Andy. I want to spend some time with Jett now."

Andy looked back at her, but Jett gave no indication she even knew anyone else was in the room. She wondered whether they knew she could still hear everything. True, it did sound like she was listening through a tunnel; vision temporarily returned, it felt like she was watching a movie scene slowly fading in. She blinked rapidly.

Andy stopped, appearing to have decided something. He looked Mr. Williams squarely in the eyes. "Okay, but please, please take care of her," he said. "She is very precious." With one last look at her, he walked hesitantly out of the room.

Mr. Williams closed the door behind him, set his watch to stopwatch mode, and directed Jett to an overstuffed chair.

"This chair right here is my favorite spot on the whole campus," he told her, crouching down beside it. "I can curl up, read a book, or look out the window to take in the beauty of nature."

He modulated his voice carefully, speaking with a gentle, soothing cadence.

"I've never shared this spot with anyone, but I want you to enjoy it now, too. I'm going to get you a blanket or two, maybe three. I bet you'll like the weight of more than one, just like me," he added, reaching into a basket near the chair and pulling out two quilts.

"My sister made these for me. My grandmother taught her how, but she did the work. They comfort me. And I think you deserve a moment of comfort. I'm going to be quiet now, but I'm going to be here, right over there at my desk. Just knock on this side table if you want my attention. It's been a full morning and I can see you need to rest."

With that, he retreated. Checking his watch as he returned to his seat behind the desk, Mr. Williams saw Jett close her eyes and burrow under the quilts.

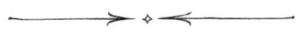

SHE WOKE UP in a magical spot. The light in the room had changed; Jett had no idea how much time had lapsed for the external world, but in her internal world it felt like a lifetime had gone by. She moved her head around slowly in an effort to sort things out, but it seemed impossible. It didn't really matter. She wanted to stay here forever.

"Ah, Jett. I see you've joined me again." Mr. Williams walked over and crouched by her side. "Did you have a nice nap?"

Jett used her fist to answer "yes," just as he had taught her—was it really only this morning?

"Can you tell me about what happened?" he asked, gesturing at the phone in her lap. "What's on your mind?"

First, she tried to speak. It was her litmus test now; she had decided she would try to speak whenever she thought of it. When her voice failed her again, she started typing.

"I was in charge of all the data collection for our team project. I had it all organized at home, mapped on our office wall. I was making progress and correlations. My parents let some people into the house and they stole our work. Not exactly, but they took pictures of EVERYTHING! Apparently, my mother thought this would be okay, but now all of our data is compromised, not to mention my privacy. What is up with THAT?"

She passed him the phone. Reading her note, Mr. Williams furrowed his brow. "I don't know, Jett. I just don't know. This *is* very odd. Can you tell me more? Who were they and why would they do that?"

Jett threw her hands up in the air. Her jaw started to flex as she unconsciously clenched her teeth and released. Clench-release-clench-release. Could he see the bewilderment pulsing at her temples? Parents were supposed to

NEEDING NORMAL 197

protect you from strangers, not give them the okay to steal your intellectual property.

In her head, so many things were competing for attention that Jett didn't know where to begin. She wanted to get it all out at once, but then she thought better of it. She was at school. This was her place of work. She should not bring in her home drama. But how could she not? Was it completely off-topic? She huffed in frustration. Jett needed to focus on the part that affected Presidio Prep—the work and her team, the Core5. She was part of them, though, and her outside life might affect both. Maybe she should tell him everything chronologically.

"It's a total mystery to me," she wrote, typing furiously. "I came home a little late, which is out of the ordinary, but my parents were yelling at my one friend in the neighborhood and there were police all over, even a detective. It looked like a scene from one of those crime shows. No one told me anything. Mother just yelled at me. But even more disturbing? Daddio looked like he was crying! What happened? How come they took the doors off my room and ALL the bathrooms?"

Mr. Williams took the phone and his eyebrows rose higher with each sentence he read. He glanced briefly at Jett, then reread it all again.

"Ooh, girl," he said, blowing out a breath. "You had quite the winter break, didn't you?"

Jett shook her head emphatically. No, she most definitely did not consider it "quite the winter break." He didn't even know the worst part yet. Could she even write it down? Jett was getting anxious. She needed to move, to let out some of this overwhelming stuff. She stood up and started to pace.

Feeling him watch her stalk around the room, like the caged albino tiger at the zoo, Jett focused on his framed photos. She especially liked the ones featuring animals and stopped right in front of a picture that looked different from all the rest: a little bit older, a little bit more personal. She thought it might be a picture of Mr. Williams, as a small boy with his dog. She touched it reverently.

"Jett, do you like dogs?"

Surprised, she spun around and looked at him. He saw tears shining in her eyes, threatening to overflow. Turning back to the picture, she shook her head. Yet, her fingers lingered on it.

It was *so* frustrating not to be able to make her meaning clear. Did he really think she *didn't* like dogs? What kind of person didn't like *dogs*? Didn't *everyone* like them, at least a little bit?

The pain of losing Yoda was so fresh Jett shook her head vigorously, trying to dispel the unbidden memories flashing in her mind. Stopping abruptly, she began typing furiously into her phone.

"It's off-topic, but OF COURSE I like dogs. On-topic? I want to know what to do about our project's compromised data."

She stopped for a moment, searching in vain for a solution, before resuming.

"Also, do you think it's possible that there is love on a team even if we aren't friends everywhere? Do you think they will still love me—forgive me even—for this breach of trust?"

A shadow of sadness crossed Mr. Williams' face as he read her message.

"Your winter break really wasn't a picnic."

He wiped a hand down his face and sighed.

"Jett, of *course* they will forgive you. I want to explain further just to make sure you understand why, but first I should speak to your parents about what happened. They need to know you have been violated, that your privacy has been breached, and that your intellectual property was compromised. I don't think they understand any of this."

What? How could they not? Seeing her bafflement, he tried again.

"Take a few moments to think about it. Meanwhile, now that I know you like dogs, I have an idea. The last place I worked—a very special place—is home to a number of very special dogs. If I can arrange it, would you like me to take you on a field trip there?"

Jett bounced on the balls of her feet, clapping and nearly jumping up and down, as she gave him a whole-body nod.

Eagerly, she shoved her phone at Mr. Williams so he could see her lockscreen image: A grinning Yoda gazing up at them, his tongue lolling. She willed him to understand how excited she was by the prospect.

"Is this your dog?" he asked with a smile.

Her face fell and lips quivered as she shook her head and took the phone back. Trying not to cry again, Jett responded: "It's Yoda. He's away at boarding school, training for work. He's not coming back. I think Ben is very sad."

Mr. Williams was puzzled.

"Well, I don't know Ben, nor do I know why Yoda isn't coming back. But what I do know is that you are very, very sad and sometimes adventures help with that. Would you like to meet some other dogs? They all went to school, too. It's a specialized training program."

Jett was nodding so much she looked like a bobble-head doll. She typed: "Like Yoda. Do you think he's there?"

"I don't think so, Jett. I don't know Yoda and I don't know where he is or what he's training to do. But I do know of these other great dogs we can visit."

Her face fell in disappointment, but then hope began to nudge at her. Mr. Williams was trying to help and even if he couldn't reconnect her with Yoda, at the very least she would get to go on an adventure. "When can we go?"

"Let me sort it out," he replied, smiling as he handed her phone back. He reached for his own phone on his desk.

"After I get it arranged, I'll have to talk to one of your parents for permission. Please—would you allow me to discuss what I learned today with them so I can get a better understanding of what happened during your break?"

Jett tensed, bunching her shoulders but nodding slowly, carefully. Some things require compromise. "Talk to my dad," she typed. "He's a lawyer. He'll understand what the police and other people were doing. Maybe he's already gone after them for trespassing. But if not, can you ask him to get on that?"

"I will," he said, with a small snort of amusement. "By the way, your day is over. Time to go home. Could you stop by here tomorrow on your way to class? Don't give up on us."

Jett nodded solemnly. Looking him directly in the eye, she used her right index finger to cross her heart. Mr. Williams hadn't given up on her. She wouldn't give up on them.

22

JETT STARTED A new routine in the period she now thought of as A.Y.—"After Yoda." Every morning, she opened her mouth and tried to speak. She figured it would be progress if she could say something—*anything*—even just make an intelligible noise for heaven's sake!

Today was Day 14 A.Y. and, faithfully, she tried to speak. Still no voice. Jett swallowed hard and gave it another go. Nope. Vocal cords definitely on hiatus. She forced air out through her nose as her jaws and fists clenched. Her knuckles turned white. Fingernails bit into her palms. This was not good. She was tired of being silent, so tired it might be time to put in her earpods and listen to her "angry" playlist.

At the "team meeting" last night, Jett, her parents, and Mr. Williams all sat in his office, reviewing the day Jett had disappeared and what it had been like. No two accounts were the same.

Mother returned home first to an unexpectedly empty home. She freaked out. She tried to text. She tried to call, but Jett wasn't answering her phone.

Daddio responded to Mother freaking out by calling in a few favors. He convinced local authorities to get involved because this was so out of character for Jett. The local authorities knew of his professional reputation as a hot-shot defense attorney. He didn't shake easily—but clearly he was shaken. His daughter wasn't around and she wasn't answering calls or responding to texts.

The house was treated like a crime scene because, for them, it had been. In their minds, her work wasn't compromised and had not been stolen. They were desperately trying to find clues to locate their daughter.

Jett, on the other hand, hadn't lost her cool that day until she realized that the chaos she saw outside had infiltrated her home. The harsh, swirling emergency lights, the unidentifiable people streaming in and out of the house, and hearing Mother attack an innocent and already hurting Ben, it all piled up. She might have been able to endure all of that, but then there was that one step that went *way* too far: Strangers examined—and photographed!—her work and all the data that had been entrusted to her. With Yoda gone, there was nowhere for her to turn. Random people with questionable morals had invaded her space. Her parents had freaked out and lashed out at Ben. And she was forced to witness her work being stolen, including unpublished data that she had yet to synthesize and share with her team. Instead of taking her breath away, the combined trauma stole her voice.

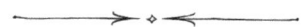

FOUR DAYS AFTER that gathering, the stressors still hadn't let go. She couldn't squeeze so much as a "hey," "yeah," or "no" out of her vocal cords. Jett's body was making choices independent of her brain. Her body had always had a mind of its own, moving in ways it didn't give her a chance to think through, much less willfully control. But throttling her voice? Why?

Jett gave up on trying to sort out that mystery, focusing instead on the meeting's conclusion: She had signatures from both parents giving permission for her special field trip with Mr. Williams. Today!

"Ah, Jett! There you are! I've been wondering when I would see you. Ready to go?" Mr. Williams looked especially enthusiastic. He must have wanted an adventure, too.

Giddy with anticipation, she followed him out to the parking lot. As they walked, Jett thought about how oddly Mother had looked at her this morning. Everything about her mood and her reactions were off. Jett had a vague sense that it had something to do with her Spiketus Rex backpack, but—why would that be?

Mr. Williams stopped next to his car and looked over the top at her, growing serious. "Before we start, I'd like to ask a favor."

Jett nodded enthusiastically.

"I just realized I won't be able to talk to you and get your quirky questions or insightful input as I drive. But that doesn't mean that we won't be having a full conversation. Okay?"

Jett tilted her head, pondering how that would be possible.

"Here's what I want you to do. Write down anything that you want to tell me or ask me. If I'm speaking too quickly, hold up your hand and I'll see it in my periphery. I'll stop speaking until you put your hand down. Want to try it?"

Jett raised her hand. Mr. Williams smiled and went silent. When she put her hand back down, Mr. Williams continued.

"Awesome! I think this is gonna work. Let's go!" Mr. Williams swung the keys around his fingers like one of those spinner toys. He was excited; she could see it.

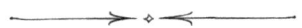

JETT WATCHED OUT the car window as they drove south past the San Francisco Zoo and continued on toward Highway One. She wondered if she would know this place or even this town they were going to visit. Oh, yeah! She was supposed to be listening to Mr. Williams. She'd gotten so wrapped up in her own thoughts that she hadn't been paying attention. Jett turned and focused on him. Apparently, he hadn't begun speaking yet. He'd been waiting for her to tune in. She ducked her head in embarrassment. Would she be graded on this?

"Jett, it's okay! Seriously, this is an educational field trip, for sure, but that doesn't mean we can't have fun, too. Do you have any idea where we're going?" Mr. Williams glanced her way and caught sight of an emphatic shake of her head.

"Okay, then. I'm going to start with a story. Once upon a time, a zillion years ago, when dinosaurs roamed... no, just kidding! But a long, long time ago, when I was doing my specialty training, I was chosen to work at this really cool place. It's so cool that I begged them to keep me there after I finished my training. They did and I got to stay until Principal Fujita found me for Presidio Prep. She asked me to be a part of realizing the school's vision and I couldn't resist. That's how I became 'Mister' Williams instead of 'Doctor.'

As they made their way down a steep curve, Jett could see a deep blue, sparkling swath of the Pacific stretched out before her. This was turning into such an amazing day! She hadn't raised her hand, so Mr. Williams carried on with his story.

"It's good, gratifying work at our school, of course, but there are days when I still really miss my old place. I miss the views and I miss the smell of the ocean. I miss the

NEEDING NORMAL 207

trees and the trails. I miss the food! Wait until you taste some of the crazy good stuff coming out of that kitchen. On most days, I miss my colleagues. The resident guests were all short-timers, but not the staff. They are steady and dedicated and most stay years and years, if not for their entire career. It's connected to the Stanford medical community, and their work is truly cutting edge."

Jett's attention was drawn away from the ocean flashing past. What kind of place was this?

"While the lodge is an amazing experience professionally, the truth is—and don't tell anyone this—I miss the canine staff most of all. I miss having such a high dog-to-human ratio and I can't wait to see if you like it, too."

Dogs? On *staff?* Like, *working? How?* The very idea sent Jett's mind into a spin. She began to tap questions frenetically into her phone.

> *Could dogs really be staff?*
> *What kind of work could they do?*
> *Did they go to boarding school first?*
> *For how long?*

Maybe this was the kind of thing Yoda would be doing after his schooling. Maybe someone there would know how to find Yoda; she hadn't had a chance to ask Ben yet.

Jett started to get even more excited as they drove through the town of Half Moon Bay. She knew where they were, but Mr. Williams kept going south. They left town, continuing past alternating ribbons of artichoke plants, brussels sprouts, and flowers. Cows grazed nearby. Jett was out of her element, out of any past experience, and she stared. Before they saw any more signs of civilization, Mr. Williams turned down an unmarked, almost hidden road that looked private and only partially paved.

The car slowed to a crawl as they approached a gate house, where Mr. Williams rolled down his window. He spoke with the guard, but with his head turned away, she couldn't hear what he said. The guard replied with open delight.

"Dr. W! So good to see you! I was excited to see your name on the list for today. I have your badge and also one for your guest. Jett, is it? Cool name!" The guard peered in the car as he handed them their badges, waggling his eyebrows at her. "You're one lucky young lady to get to know about the secret lair." Startled to be addressed with such familiarity by a stranger, Jett looked to Mr. Williams for reassurance. He shrugged nonchalantly as the guard continued speaking to her. Didn›t this man know about stranger danger?

"This is home to some of the greatest secret superheroes and their sidekicks! I bet that's why he brought you. Are you thinking of becoming one, like this guy here?" he asked, gesturing at Mr. Williams with an elbow.

Jett froze. She didn't know how to respond. Superheroes and sidekicks? The guard didn't seem to notice that she remained silent.

"Well, it's a cool place to be if you do." He backed away from the car, picked up a clipboard, and made some notations as he waved them on. "You're all signed in. See you guys later!"

As they made their way down the gravel road, Jett resumed typing. What was this place called? The Secret Lair? Like in Batman? Superheroes and sidekicks? What was the guard talking about?

She paused, wondering if she should write down her next thoughts. Should he be medicated or at least supervised? But—what if he was right? Did superheroes exist? She *thought* that was made up. Was Mr. Williams *really* one? And if so, why was he trying to hide it? Why was it secret? She had always wondered if he had superpowers.

They made their way around a bend in the road and her mouth fell open. Waves crashed stubbornly against jagged bluffs. Gnarled cypress turned away from the wind blowing off the ocean. Majestic redwoods climbed the hillsides beyond them. A breathtaking wood-shingled lodge appeared to grow out of the manicured lawn, surrounded by colorful flower beds. Stone pillars held exposed beams aloft, welcoming visitors. Double doors fitted with wrought iron and stained glass opened to a grand, but inviting, lobby. Was this the *place*? As the car came to a stop right in front, she looked down at her notes. Now, her questions seemed so...basic. This place looked like the perfect spot to wrestle with your deepest questions, reconsider your life plans, and sketch out new paths. Jett was in awe.

Mr. Williams shifted into park, switched off the engine, and opened the door with an enormous sigh of contentment. The scent of salt air and coastal sage rushed in as he got out and stretched his arms and legs.

Jett saw a few teens and adults sitting at picnic tables, quietly talking. Were they on a field trip too? They seemed so relaxed. Had she ever been so relaxed? She pondered for a long moment before remembering: yes, she had. She had worn those facial expressions and had held her body loosely, in postures like those, before "normal" became a central question, before she had to prove that she was. Would they know she wasn't? She tried to imitate their relaxation for a moment as she climbed out of the car, but when she looked again at the lodge, she remembered the dogs. Instantly, Jett started bouncing up and down on the balls of her feet, eager to go inside.

Mr. Williams held one of the double doors open for her, inviting Jett to step inside ahead of him. In front of a wall of windows, people congregated in small clusters—adults, teens, and *dogs*! *So many dogs!* There were almost as many dogs as there were adults. He hadn't been exaggerating *at all*!

She turned to Mr. Williams with a stunned look on her face, mouth open, eyes wide and sparkling. He beamed at Jett as her bouncing shifted to full-body rocking.

"That's right. Ask away."

Quickly she added to her list:

TELL ME EVERYTHING

And pressed the phone into his hands. Jett shifted her weight from foot to foot, grabbed the skin above her clavicle and, in a rapid rhythm, she started to pinch and knead it. Knuckles hitting her clavicle sounded like a drum. It was an unconscious decision. Her body needed to release this tension.

Unphased by this, Mr. Williams began to peruse her note. He stopped reading as a stunning young woman headed their way, a dog at her side. While the lady reached out to shake Mr. Williams' hand in greeting, the big, black dog continued past him to Jett, who was still in full motion. He studied her for a moment, then looked at the woman, who nodded silent permission at him. The dog nudged Jett's leg once and then leaned into her.

Jett stopped pinching her neck. Feeling the comfort of his body pressure as he leaned insistently against her, she felt connected and understood, accepted. This made no logical sense to her but it didn't have to. It was still real. Jett started to cry and smile at the same time.

She had never seen a dog exactly like this before. He was big—huge, even. He was muscular and obviously strong, but yet somehow gentle and so very aware. He looked like a Clifford-sized version of a scottie dog. Huh. What kind of dog looked like a giant scottie?

"Jett, meet Gus and my colleague, Sylvia," Mr. Williams said, still smiling broadly at her. "Sylvia, meet my favorite student, Jett."

Emerald eyes examined Jett and Gus, but Jett barely noticed. She offered a small wave in their general direction and refocused on Gus.

Sylvia stepped away from Mr. Williams and spoke softly to Jett. "Hi there. Seems like Gus wants to work with you. I hope it's all right that I released him into your care."

Jett nodded vigorously and let her hand drop to touch Gus for the first time. She let out a long breath she hadn't known she was holding. He felt like velvet. Tentatively, she began to skritch behind one of his enormous ears.

"I'm grateful you brought my friend here back to visit us," Sylvia said. "If you don't mind, we're going to stay in this front room, which we like to call the Atrium. See those comfy chairs over there? Dr. W and I are going to sit and chat for a bit, but you and Gus are free to wander. Just stay in this room, okay? Later, we can all go on a tour and have lunch. How does that sound?"

Utterly enthralled with Gus, Jett didn't respond. Sylvia glanced at Mr. Williams, who waited briefly before reaching out to touch Jett's elbow. She tore her attention away from Gus and looked at him.

"Just checking in, Jett. Did you hear Sylvia? We're going to hang out here for a bit. You can stay with Gus, but don't wander from this room. Let me know if you agree."

She smiled and gave him a little nod, both hands now running through Gus's coat. Her whole posture had changed. She felt relaxed and content; why would she want a tour? Couldn't she just stay here all day?

The two adults walked toward chairs facing a bank of windows overlooking the bluff and the crashing waves. They took in the view of the ocean briefly before sitting down.

Jett watched them go and felt Gus shift. Did he want to go somewhere? He was a very patient dog, she thought. Cautiously, she took a step.

Gus matched it.

She took another and he took one as well. It was as if they were in sync. Jett looked around, but no one was watching. Didn't anyone see how amazing this was? She wandered around the room and Gus wandered, too, staying by her side, matching her step for step. Without thinking, Jett reached down and patted him approvingly. "Look at you," she murmured. "You're a good boy, Gus. How did you learn to walk with me?"

Gus looked up into her face as if he was going to speak back. He even opened his mouth. But of course he couldn't talk like Jett could.

Realizing that her voice was back, her head whipped up. She could talk! Vocal cord vacation was over and she hopped in excitement.

Gus barked at her unexpected movement and tried to match her moves. Jett laughed in delight. Mr. Williams and Sylvia looked up to see Jett and Gus running toward them, excitement obvious in their every move.

"Hi, Sylvia! I'm Jett Harper. Thank you for allowing me time with Gus. May I please keep playing with him? I'm sorry he barked. I think I scared him when I jumped, but I got so excited and my body just reacted. My body does that: it just reacts. Sometimes I think it has a mind of its own."

With raised eyebrows, Sylvia turned to Mr. Williams. "Of course you can! But Dr. Williams was just telling me about your silence. He said you couldn't speak right now, but I think you speak very well. Can I ask you a question about that? When you weren't speaking, did you have a choice or did your body choose for you?"

"Great question," Jett said. "At first, I chose not to speak, but after a while my body chose for me and then I couldn't speak. I tried and tried. It was awful. Now I can." A shadow of doubt clouded her face. "Will that happen again, though? How do I make sure it doesn't?"

"I don't know, Jett," Mr. Williams offered, "but I think we should tell your parents. They're going to be so excited."

Jett shook her head. "Can we wait just a little bit? I want to be sure my voice stays, and I want to hang out with Gus. Can we go on that tour now? Does he live here? I want to see where he lives."

Sylvia and Mr. Williams rose in unison to begin the tour. As they walked through the building, Jett peppered them both with questions, growing increasingly intrigued the more she learned.

"What is this place called?" she asked.

Mr. Williams and Sylvia looked at each other before answering in unison. "The Learning Lodge."

That made sense, Jett thought. She was already learning here.

As the day drew to a close, Sylvia and Mr. Williams exchanged a meaningful look. He cleared his throat to draw Jett's attention away from Gus.

"Hey, Jett. It's time to go."

Her face fell and she moved closer to Gus, shaking her head.

"Jett, really, I need to get back."

Her head drooped.

"I've discussed it with Sylvia and your parents and, if you would like, you *could* stay here with Gus for a learning intensive," he offered.

Her eyes opened wide as she stared at him.

"Would you like to take a bit of time and study here? You would have to do all of your regular schoolwork and the extra work from being here—extra tests and classes—but Gus and Sylvia will be here and I will visit with your parents, if you want. Your parents gave me a suitcase full of things for you in case you chose to stay. It was important to your dad that you got to make the decision about staying. What do you think?"

She couldn't believe her luck!

"Can Gus stay with me the whole time? Like even in one of those guest rooms?"

Sylvia smiled at her.

"Usually Gus is mine, Jett, but I'm happy to share him with you while you are here," she said, dropping a hand onto the dog's head. "I'll lend him to you if you participate in *all* the work. How does that sound?"

Jett thought she might burst with happiness. "Did you say all of my regular work plus extra tests, too? Will you share my results with me?"

Both of them nodded at her.

"When can I begin?"

Beaming with pleasure, Dr. W assured her, "You already have."

23

JETT KNEW FOUR THINGS:

> *1. Her voice came back talking to Gus.*
> *2. She had limited time to sort out what that meant.*
> *3. Her parents were coming. Today. They may even be on their way.*
> *4. Unless she sorted out why she could speak again, she couldn't avoid the triggers.*

It would happen again.

Jett stared out the windows, standing perfectly still with Gus by her side, and looked at the angry waves pummeling the bluffs. Lost in doubt, she struggled to figure out what to do. She wanted—no, she *needed*—to know with absolute certainty that she would continue to have a voice after she went home without Gus.

She tried breathing deep. She tried to be brave. Sylvia had been so generous to share Gus with her over the past month. But soon Jett would be on her own again. She could feel Sylvia's kind—but piercing—eyes following them everywhere. Jett didn't know if she was ready. She didn't want to go home. Not yet. Sylvia wasn't intrusive, but she always seemed to know where Jett and Gus were at any given moment. Jett felt her constant tracking like the weight of having the doors removed at home. At least here, though, she could go behind closed doors. But the lodge also had cameras. Jett was under no illusion that she had any real privacy. That didn't really bother her, though, because she couldn't think of one reason she needed it. What habits did she have that required secrecy? Wasn't it normal to sort out things that confused you or just plain interested you? Couldn't she be normal for just a few days, without trying, without having to think about it all the time?

Jett reached out for Gus, who never left her side. He accepted her as-is; he didn't care what humans may think. Jett was normal to him. She was grateful for his ability to let her just be, well, Jett.

She felt Sylvia approaching even before she heard her voice. "Hey, Jett. Today is the day we share some deep thoughts with you. Are you ready?"

Twining her fingers into Gus's fur, Jett turned away from the storm-tossed waves outside the windows.

"Who will be leading these sessions? Dr. M or Dr. J? I like them best," asked Jett. "They're easy to understand and don't seem to mind when I ask too many questions."

"Both have taken a special interest in your progress," Sylvia said. "I'm curious, though. Has everyone here supported your willingness to learn and worked to make sure you understand? No one has made you hesitant to ask questions, have they?"

Jett shook her head. "No one here. It's like you guys invite my questions, like you want me to understand. And no one laughs at me when I don't. That's new to me, having unfiltered access to knowledge. Is that why you call this place the Learning Lodge?"

Sylvia offered a sad smile. "Yes, that is part of why we chose that name. We believe learning is key to the application of knowledge, and application is key to contentment. Our goal is to help our guests be content."

Jett was surprised. "Huh. Most people try to be happy. How is contentment better?"

That brought Sylvia's smile up a notch. "Jett, your questions prove that you truly are one-of-a-kind brilliant. I don't want to spoil today's conversations by leaving Dr. J or Dr. M out of my reply to that. Can we wait for them? They'll likely have opinions on that issue, too. But personally I love that contentment includes all of my emotional states without declaring only one as valid."

That was a new way of looking at it, Jett thought. All emotions are valid and worthy of being expressed. That made sense, now that she thought about it, but it was still surprising.

"I think you've got something there," she told Sylvia. "I can't wait to discuss this today. Is today also the day my parents are coming?"

Jett noticed that Sylvia's intense observation sharpened as she answered. "Your parents actually should be here soon. Are you looking forward to seeing them?"

Jett shrugged. She wasn't sure. Seeing them? Yeah, maybe. But if that meant leaving here…

She looked down at Gus just as he tilted his head up and grinned at her. At least, she thought it was a grin. Tongue lolling and mouth open—she wasn't sure how else to describe it. Jett ruffled his fur as her eyes started to fill with tears. Was she ready to leave the Learning Lodge? Jett blew out a heavy breath. She tried to allow emotions to flow through her body, so they wouldn't steal her voice again. A fresh wave of uncertainty flooded in.

Just then, Dr. M and Dr. J arrived. Dr. M, a tall woman with a wild mane of fiery hair, greeted them in her enthusiastic style. Dr. J, a short, round man with a neatly-trimmed beard, basically the polar opposite of Dr. M, spoke first. "Ready to talk about typical and normal?"

"What?" Jett said, startled. "I thought we were talking about contentment."

With a pointed look at the doctors, Sylvia deflected. "Maybe we can start with contentment versus happiness and then progress to normal and typical. How does that sound?"

The group moved into a learning room that looked nothing like the classrooms at Presidio Prep. It actually reminded Jett of the office at home. She loved it. Everyone sat down in comfortable chairs and loungers while Gus stayed at her feet. Jett noted that there were no other guests around today; it was just her and the team. She loved how they didn't waste time with idle chatter, instead getting right into the conversation that Sylvia had foreshadowed. The discussion was so engrossing, she needed to take notes.

Jett stood up and went to the white board. She wrote on it, "Happy vs. Content," highlighting each word in a different color.

Dr. J, who behaved as the senior member of the team, looked at her approvingly.

"Thanks, Jett. It's also important to me that we get to 'typical' and 'normal' today. Can you put those two words up as well?" Jett grabbed two other colors and added them to the board. She waited for more input. When none came, she returned to her seat—and Gus—as the discussion resumed.

Ninety minutes later, Jett felt saturated with new concepts, as if her head might explode. As she stared at the overflow of notes on the whiteboard, she put up her hand in the universal sign for stop.

"Wait. Wait a minute here! Let me see if I've got this straight. What you're telling me is, happy and sad and everything else I feel *all* can be part of contentment? You're saying all the emotions are valid. 'Typical' is comparative, while 'normal' is personally subjective. Are you telling me normal doesn't matter?!?"

"No, I'm suggesting just the opposite," Dr. M said. "*Typical* doesn't matter. And 'normal' is whatever you experience and accept it to be. In other words, however you experience your life—*that's* 'normal.'"

Dr. J tried for a more empathetic tone. "I know 'normal' has been your quest, but what I really want you to know is that you *are* normal. You always have been and you always will be. *You* are normal and so is every person you meet. Everyone reflects their own personal 'normal,' even when it's not the same as someone else's 'normal,' and even when it's not 'typical.'"

Jett was still struggling to process this when her parents walked purposefully into the room—Daddio warm and Mother icy. That did not bode well. And their timing was terrible, she thought, coming just when she believed herself to be on the brink of something crucial.

Curious and not a little bit anxious about what they would think of all of this, Jett wondered whether she would get to stay longer or whether they would force her to leave. She wanted to keep debating, to keep learning right where she was.

But—wait. What about her Core5 at Presidio Prep? What about the Love Project? What about Ben? Was anyone checking on him? Had Mother even apologized? Could Ben tell her how Yoda was doing at his school? Did dogs get grades?

Jett felt her voice constricting and her panic expanding. She was unsure how this would go, but at the same time she was glad for all the new knowledge, especially the confirmation she was normal. Jett wondered just how relieved Mother would be when she learned her daughter wasn't broken. Would all those stress lines magically be erased from her face?

Daddio jumped into the growing silence first. "Hi, I'm Joe Harper and this is my wife, Kathy. We're happy to be here. I've heard only good things about this place." Then Daddio looked right at her. "I've missed you, Bug," he said, emotion clogging his tone. She was surprised to see his eyes were brimming with tears. Jett tilted her head at this unusually public display of emotion. Had Daddio been talking to a doctor about emotions, too? Did he know about contentment versus happiness? That would be so cool!

That's when Mother derailed everything.

"Thank you for your work with our daughter. I'm looking forward to learning about your assessments and treatment plans moving forward," she said crisply. "I'm hoping you can help us sort through the vagaries of PTSD. Neither of us have any experience as parents of a child who has been through trauma. My work as a therapist mostly deals with depression and anxiety. Nothing like this at all."

Although some staff members greeted this with neutral expressions, Jett saw that others were stunned and struggled to recover their poker faces. She loved observing such nuances and wondered both whether they agreed with Mother and just when she had contracted Post Traumatic Stress Disorder. That diagnosis was news to her.

She wasn't surprised, however, to hear Mother in therapist mode. Did she think they were her colleagues? Would she try to impress them with her connections and personal practice? Jett hoped not. It would be so embarrassing to have Mother take over like she was an authority here, too. Would she be open to learning anything at the Learning Lodge?

Dr. M recovered first and took the situation in hand.

"Thank you for coming. Let's all have a seat, shall we?" She waited while her parents settled in. "I'd like to begin by letting you know right away that Jett doesn't have PTSD. I'm sure that's a big relief!" Dr. M smiled and everyone waited for Jett's parents to show signs of visible relief. They didn't. Jett wondered why.

Dr. J took a turn. "Hi, Mr. and Mrs. Harper. I'm known simply as Dr. J around here. Let's get caught up on what Jett has taught us over the last month and then, if she's ready, she can tell you what she's learned. How does that sound?"

Daddio nodded and Mother frowned as she crossed her arms. Jett wondered what confused her. This seemed pretty basic to her.

"Excuse me," Mother interjected. "Did you say what Jett taught *you*? *That's* where you'd like to start? How about we skip that and get straight into her diagnosis and how to fix her."

Jett's team looked around at each other briefly before Sylvia stepped up to the plate. "Mrs. Harper, I'm Sylvia, Jett's mentor. As you know from the information we sent earlier, we have an exceptionally qualified team here supporting your daughter. So, we'd like not to skip over the important contributions Jett has made to our Lodge. Are you ready to listen? I promise we will also give you time to be heard."

Jett watched Mother's stress lines deepen as her posture went from contained to rigid. Apparently, she wasn't used to anyone challenging her. Jett watched as Dr. M, Dr. J, and Sylvia all intentionally relaxed. Unconsciously, Jett reached for Gus. He sat up and put his head in her lap. She worked to slow her breathing and match it to the rhythm of petting Gus. She looked up in time to see Daddio assessing the situation.

His smile broadened. Apparently, he was enjoying this. He caught her watching and winked. Jett loved Daddio and smiled back at him as understanding flooded into her. *She loved someone!* Holy revelations, Batman! Maybe the security guard had been right. Maybe there really were superheroes and sidekicks here at the Learning Lodge.

A few hours later, Daddio was in full revelry. He seemed to be absorbing everything he was learning with delight. But Mother was a different story. She resisted every part of the team's message, refusing to accept that Jett could be normal and not typical. Mother spoke candidly, without regard for how her words would land. Her pitch and tone rose precipitously.

"Are you sure nothing happened to cause her to be this way? She's not … " Mother glanced at Jett. She seemed to take a moment and consider her daughter carefully, looking for signs of something.

Of what? Jett wondered.

Mother turned back to the Learning Lodge staff. She stage whispered, as if that would stop Jett from hearing her words or feeling their impact. "She's not broken? Data proves this? That Jett is normal *and* atypical? Isn't that an oxymoron? And most importantly, are you telling me she will always be this way?"

Many beats of silence followed. Finally, Dr. J answered.

"Wow. I'm so glad you spoke your mind and I'm still kind of reeling. I'm not sure where to start." He looked over at Sylvia, handing her the baton. "Sylvia, you're the resident expert in normal and typical. Would you like to address that part?"

Syliva gathered her thoughts for a moment before focusing on the Harpers. "As we've said, we don't think Jett's typical. She is extremely bright, curious, and focused on things that interest her. She puts together information in fascinating and brilliant ways and her empathy is off the charts."

Mother interrupted. "Wait a minute. I agree she's bright. I agree she can be hyper-focused. But her empathy 'off the charts?' I haven't seen that and if you're leading us down the path I think you are—don't people with her diagnosis usually have less empathy? She feels less, not more. She is a drama queen, sure, but I think it's because she's so privileged."

Jett's body shrunk in on itself. Wow. Mother really had no clue how her words were landing—or maybe she just didn't care. Jett knew this and so did Gus on some level; he maneuvered himself on top of her, using his body like a living weighted blanket to soothe and ground the frayed edges of her raw nerves.

The conversation slowed as Dr. M brought Jett a glass of water, blocking her view of anyone else. Jett focused on her face as Dr. M spoke quietly. "Jett, take a sip." As she moved in beside her, Jett saw Daddio taking in the new ways she was receiving support. Jett was embarrassed and ashamed. What did Daddio think of her now, now that he knew she needed this different level of care?

Jett refocused on the broader discussion, noticing that Sylvia and Dr. J were deliberately carrying the conversation to give her a few moments to recover.

"Yes, actually, that is exactly what we are saying," Dr. J was telling Mother. "Jett is normal because normal is a personal subjective. Typical, on the other hand, is a comparative subjective and therefore not at all the same. Your brilliant daughter is not broken, nor will she always be—as you say, 'this way'—because she is a growing, developing, human being interested in learning. So, no, definitively—Jett is not broken. Our hope for her is that she will continue to develop and use the tools that serve her. Our hope is that she will continue to express herself and not let things unintentionally bottle up and steal her voice. Our hope is that she will model normal and not typical, in a world expecting normal and typical, and not feel less than. No one is *ever* always one way. What we want to emphasize here is Jett isn't broken. She is normal. She may not be typical, but she is normal."

Mother's face had flushed dangerously as he spoke. When he finished his thoughts, she exploded.

"But she *is* less than! *Disabled* is less than. It means she needs help just to fit in."

Dr. M lost his composure and exploded right back. "Why is fitting in more important than standing out? When did different start to mean less than?"

Tentatively, Jett raised her hand. All eyes turned to

her. In the hours since her parents' arrival, she had yet to speak. In truth, they had not heard her voice in all the many weeks since Yoda went away. She looked Mother in the eyes. Remembering Mother's low growl of "not normal" on the first day of school, Jett squared her shoulders. She pulled her body up so she was sitting extra tall. Enough was enough. "May I speak?"

Her team members nodded encouragingly.

Jett applied a laser focus on Mother.

"I am normal and I am smart. And, being smart, I can learn how to mimic 'typical.'" She spat out the last word out like it was an insult, crossed her arms, and continued to stare Mother down.

The room went still. A boom of clapping broke the silence. Applauding, Daddio stood up.

"Jett, you are smart. You are brilliant. And what's more, you are determined. I've never met anyone who tried harder. I want you to teach me how to support you better because you, my girl, can do great things. Typical be damned. I love that you stand out. Can I just hug you?" He moved toward her; Gus leaned into her from the side. Jett felt herself relax in Daddio's arms.

Mother destroyed the moment. "I think we're done here. This is not what I expected, and I'm not sure how it was even helpful," she said, standing and beginning to stride toward the door. "A month. You've had our daughter one month and filled her head with nonsense. But it's okay. We're going home now and I'll fix it. Expect my call. We will talk."

Jett was in shock. She looked at Daddio; clearly, he was stunned. That was it, then. She was going home now. Acidic bile rose in her throat. Jett was sickened—and angry. Mother had learned nothing. Daddio and Jett? They had learned everything that mattered. This was it. She just had to prove her case in the real world. She would mimic typical.

Jett was more determined than ever to not only get an 'A' on the Love Project, but to win all the Freshman Faire Awards. After all, she knew what love was. It was her Daddio. It was learning things, like she had in this place. And, it was a pup.

24

PRESIDIO PREP'S LIBRARY was located in a building away from the main activities. If you asked the librarians, they would agree this was intentional. Jett didn't care one way or the other. She was committed to picking up where she left off, which meant interviewing every member of the Core5, one by one. She was just glad to have a quiet place to meet up with Andy before officially getting back into classes. She wanted to collect more data for the project and see her second everywhere friend.

Andy looked up when he heard footsteps approaching. Jett watched him take her in.

He raised a hand in languid greeting as a slow smile lit his eyes and traveled to his mouth. He looked happy to see her.

She was right on time and felt as eager as Andy looked. Jett immediately looked down to check out his socks. Today Andy wore hearts. The Ed Hardy tattoo kind of hearts.

On. His. Socks! And a grey beanie pulled snuggly over his ears per his usual non-uniform uniform. His button-down shirt was crisp and his soft Levi's kissed the top of his "old man shoes," as Ruby called them. Jett thought he had the look of someone who knew things. Lots of things. Maybe more than your average grown-up. To her, Andy looked prepared. He sat up as she approached.

"Hey, Jett! I'm glad to see you. I was beginning to worry you weren't coming back. No one knew where you went after your field trip with Dr. Williams. Everything okay?"

She nodded and smiled. Jett was clear now: Andy was her second friend outside of class. She wondered if Sam would be her third everywhere friend. Unless—would all of that have changed when she went away without explanation? Jett shrugged at the thought, realizing there was nothing she could do about that right now. She was learning to focus on things she could control, like the collection of data. Looking into Andy's open face, she smiled. He was a good second friend. And now it was time to get down to business. Settling into the chair across from him, she pulled out her phone and opened up the notes app.

"Ever since reading your initial paper, I've been wanting to learn more about love from you. Will you tell me what you know? Can I take notes?"

Andy sat up straighter. "Sure, but I think I included everything I know in the paper." He took off his hat and ran his fingers through his hair distractedly.

Jett watched, transfixed by the texture. It was the first time she realized hair and fur had similarities. Andy's hair was kind of like thick, dark fur. It looked a little bit like Gus's dense coat, even similar in color. Would it also feel like velvet? Could she run her fingers through...

"I've been thinking a lot about it and I don't know how much more I can add, but maybe it would help if you ask me questions," he suggested. "Maybe I can clarify something that doesn't make sense like I think it does."

Andy didn't seem to notice that her mind had wandered. Good thing she hadn't reached out to test her theory. That would be weird. Would that be weird? Yeah. Definitely weird.

Refocusing, she switched to her phone's voice memo app.

"Okay if I just record our conversation instead? That way I can just listen to it later and pull out what I learned."

He nodded and Jett pressed "record."

"First of all, I thought your paper was fascinating. You mentioned so many people! Can you help me understand how all these different family members give you love? Is it all the same or all different? My family is a lot smaller. Does that mean I get less love?"

Andy shrugged again, struggling to explain.

"For me, it does all come down to family. My Dadi and Dada live with us, so we spend lots of time together. My other grandparents live in Michigan. Nani and Nana talk about moving closer when Nana retires, but they're really involved in their community, so we might just continue to go visit them each summer."

Andy went on to explain how in Indian culture, families are extremely tight-knit across generations and throughout their local community. "We call all the grown-ups we love and respect 'Auntie' and 'Uncle,' even if they're not related to us by blood," he said. "They're all considered family. We kind of adopt each other—not officially or anything, but we look out for each other."

Part of that, he explained, is being intentionally thoughtful.

"Even as kids, we try to find ways to show love," he said. "In our family, we show love by doing things for each other—like my Dadi making us meals and Dada reading to each one of us, every day. I love that. He's got like six books going at once."

Excited, he gestured at Jett's phone. "That could be something. Maybe reading is a love thing—like a love language or something! He's always doing it."

Immediately, Jett thought of the conversation she'd had with Ben months ago. Love language! Ben had told her to research love languages. Now Andy was talking about it!

"Yes, that's *exactly* it!" she said. "My neighbor Ben talked about love languages. Let's look this up."

They spent the rest of the hour looking up love languages and learning about the theory. It kind of made sense, but Andy seemed concerned. His Dada, he told Jett, believed in lifelong learning. Kids and young adults were expected to focus on getting a college education, including going on to graduate school, to make the family proud.

"I've always thought if I don't go down that road, I'd be letting our family down and not showing them love," he said, as worry lines creased his brow. "Kind of like when I decided to Americanize my name. My Mom was so sad that she cried for like a month. Everyone calls me by my real name outside of school. Do you think if I go another route professionally, I'll be letting my family down and not showing them all the love I have for them?"

But Jett was caught on the term "Americanize."

"Wait. What? Isn't Andy your name? You write it on your papers. If it's not Andy, then what is it? Why would you change it? What does 'Americanize' even mean? Aren't you American? Why would you want to be if you aren't?"

Andy sighed and glanced uncomfortably at Jett's phone, which was still recording. He cleared his throat.

"I—uh—didn't mean to say so much." He looked Jett in the eyes. "You're not going to share this anywhere, right? All of this is just for you to sort through and we can talk about it before you bring it to the group. Promise me that you'll keep this private."

"Absolutely," she said immediately. "I promise that all your family details are private. I just want to use the love languages part for the project. But I do want to understand what you've been telling me. Can we start with your real name? Why would you be called something else at school? Is your name a secret? Because of your family or heritage or something?"

Andy ran his fingers through his hair again as he studied Jett. After a few moments, he seemed to reach a decision.

"My grandparents are all from the same region of India called Gujarat. They didn't know each other because it's a state with over 60 million people. But their families knew *of* each other. And both families immigrated to the United States about the same time. My parents met in their English class at Harvard. It wasn't an arranged marriage. They fell in love freshman year and have been together ever since. After graduating, they had a big three-day Indian wedding and everything. They went to grad school, they both have good jobs, and they live fulfilling lives."

"Don't you mean 'happy lives?'"

"Nope. I mean fulfilling," Andy said. "We don't really focus on 'happy.' My Nani—that's my Mom's mom, says: 'Happy is like a butterfly. If you don't focus on it, it comes and lands on your shoulder. But if you try to catch it or trap it, you will always be chasing and could be led down a path you don't want to go.'"

Andy laughed under his breath. "I'm not sure what she means all the time, but Mom just tells us to focus on being fulfilled, instead, because that's what has brought her so much happiness and love."

Jett put up a hand and closed her eyes, beckoning him to stop for a moment. She wasn't really thinking; she just wanted to take a moment to feel the weight and truth of the words. When she was ready, she put her hand back down and opened her eyes.

"I like your Nani and your Mom. They have good ideas. Do you think they would love me?"

"I bet they would!" he said, smiling broadly at her. "I've told them about our Core5 and they already think we're a good team. Mom and Dadi wanted to know when you all are coming over."

Jett was thrilled. "Really? Come over, outside of school? But what will we call you, if you aren't called Andy at home?"

"That right there is my problem," Andy said ruefully. "I'm not sure I'm ready for my two worlds to collide yet. Here, I'm Andy. There, I'm Anand. Here, I can eat whatever is meatless at the cafe. There, I eat the best khichdi and my Mom's awesome smoothies. Here, it's conceivable that I'll work on my mad baking skills and maybe one day win that baking show on the Food Network. But at home, it's out of the question. They think I'm wasting my time on baking. It's what I love, but not good for *who* I love."

There was so much to unpack in that last phrase that Jett just shook her head in confusion. She decided to start simple.

"First of all, I'm gonna need you to say your name again—your real one, because I think it sounds cool! And I want to call you by your real name when you're ready, so I'm gonna have to practice."

Jett saw a new light enter Andy's eyes.

"Second, you can bake? Like really *bake*, bake? As in, fancy-schmancy *desserts*?" Andy's versatility amazed her. "How is doing what you love not good enough for who you love? Is it illegal or immoral or something? My Dad says not to do those things, the illegal and immoral ones. I keep looking for a list so I can review it and make sure I'm not going in the wrong direction, but I haven't found one. You're telling me *baking* would be on that list?" Her eyes grew huge at the implications.

Andy's smile dissolved into laughter—a lot of it. He was wiping at his eyes and grinning and still laughing as he tried to explain.

"Baking would not make that list, no," he said. "But it also would not be something that might change the world, something that would save lives. I'm supposed to be a doctor, not a pastry chef."

This wasn't helping to resolve her confusion. "Can't you be both?" she asked. "I mean seriously. Couldn't your baking put you through medical school or something? Couldn't you be a baking doctor? And don't think I've forgotten about your name. Please teach me."

"I will, but first let's talk about love," Andy said, growing serious again. "We can probably use that love languages thing as a structure for our project. But tell me this honestly: Do you think it's more loving to be true to myself and who I feel I am, or is it more loving to reflect how my family sees me and what they want me to be?"

Jett thought back to her Learning Lodge discussions about happiness versus contentment versus fulfillment. She thought about all the different ways love was expressed. She thought about Sam and Andy both trusting her to guard their secrets and she thought about being true to herself versus what others expect. Jett looked him in the eye and made a decision. She decided to trust him back.

"Andy, here is what I know," she said, letting out a deep breath. "We're not talking about illegal or immoral. We're talking about you being happy, content, or fulfilled, and I don't think those are mutually exclusive. I'm happy when I'm content. I'm content when I feel fulfilled. Being loving with my family means trying to speak to them in ways they can hear me. It sometimes means doing things for them so they can feel appreciated even when I don't understand."

Something clicked in her brain as she told Andy that.

"Which means I have to go shopping with my Mom, maybe even ask her to take me shopping," she grimaced. "That would be a loving thing for me to do. And you can bake *and* be a doctor. I know it. But you also can keep your cool name versus telling everyone your name is Andy. Andy is just so—*Andy*!" She made a face.

Andy laughed again, then got busy teaching Jett how to say his real name. As she struggled to say Anand right, he tried not to laugh but his chuckle betrayed his mirth.

"What? What are you laughing at?"

"You, Jett. You make me laugh. And I'm so glad we're part of the same Core5. I'm going to change my school name to my real name. Thank you for helping me sort that out."

Jett nodded in acknowledgement. "Okay, but can you give me a few days or even a week to practice first? I want to get it right."

He let out a low chuckle, but agreed. Andy touched her shoulder as they stood up to leave. "Come on. Let's get out of here. You *do* know, you *already* know all about this love thing, right?"

"No, I don't know that. I *know* I don't know," she said. "But I'm willing to learn." Tomorrow was her first day back in class and she *needed* to learn.

Andy stopped in his tracks, put a hand on each of her shoulders, and looked Jett in the eyes. "I think you know so much more than you think you do."

25

TODAY WOULD BE monumental. Jett could feel it, just like her first day at Presidio Prep. Butterflies danced in her stomach. She didn't know whether she was excited or scared or both, maybe. Yeah, it was both. This was her first full day back on campus, the first day in class since returning from the Learning Lodge. She knew more about herself than she'd ever known before. For example, she *knew* she was normal, just not typical.

Jett wondered if her peers knew the difference—or whether they even cared. Did they know they're normal, too? Were they all typical? She certainly didn't think so. Maybe she could talk the rest of her Core5 into getting tested. What Jett really wanted to know, though, was how they would pull off a win at the Freshmen Faire. Had she been replaced? What progress had they made? Who wrote the manual on how to be a loving person? Where did they get the data?

The Foundations classroom had been transformed. Instead of four neat rows of orderly desks, round tables, each with seating for five students, took up the space. Each of the teams had their own spot to facilitate working together. But Jett was full of nervous energy and couldn't sit. She paced around the perimeter of the room, watching people get settled. All she knew for certain was that her Core5 had very little time left to get this project wrapped up. They had roughly six weeks to compile the data, two weeks to put together the final paper, and another week or so to sort out a presentation. Then it was time for the Freshman Faire and this is what she knew: they *had* to win.

Jett thought she finally had figured out her *Breakfast Club* cast. Andy was the Brain, Sam the Rebel, Carlos the Athlete, and Ruby the Princess. That left one spot for her. She frowned. Wait a minute. Basket Case? Hmmm. What did that even mean?

No, she categorically rejected that label. Jett decided to recast "the Basket Case" as "the Misunderstood." She could claim that. For sure. After all, wasn't it the story of her life?

If she was correct, no one knew what was going on in her life and possibly not with the project, either. It was time to fix that.

Jett straightened her shoulders and walked purposefully toward the other members of her Core5. She approached their table. Her mind whirled behind her calm facade.

What exactly did they know? How should she play this? Was she still in charge of data? Did she need to take on more? What did they expect? Jett really needed to sort out her role here. She was tired of being misunderstood.

"'Manita!" Carlos exclaimed. "I missed you! Where've you been? Are you mad at me? I want you to know, I love the gift you gave me! What I don't love is you disappearing. But, hey, I heard you can talk again!" He looked sideways at Andy and then focused back on Jett. "Is that true? Why did you talk to Andy and not to me?" Hamming it up, Carlos got down on his knees in front of her, hands clasped pleadingly. "Why, Manita? Why?"

"Carlos, cut it," Sam interjected. "Give our girl time to speak. Seriously, dude, how do you expect her to answer when you don't give her room to talk?"

Jett felt all eyes on her as she mustered her courage. She'd been debating what to tell them, of course. Just based on Mother's reaction to the Learning Lodge, she knew not everyone would be supportive. Should she describe why people spent time there, or that she now had regular virtual lessons with her team there? How much information did she owe them?

"Girl, where you been?" Sam asked, interrupting her thoughts. "Ruby's been a total bee-otch. You know she's hard to stomach at the best of times, but you should see how she is when she can't find something out! It was like you being gone was about *her*. In the world according to Princess Ruby, *everything* revolves around her!"

Ruby tossed her hair as if in agreement. Sam smirked and rolled her eyes at her. "See what I mean? Ruby's a *total* P.I.T.A.!"

Ruby pouted and crossed her arms in a huff. Everyone sat, as if this was the cue to settle in.

Jett had missed these little dramas; she found herself relaxing as this one played out. She was learning so much just by observing, like that Carlos had been worried, Sam wanted to protect Jett's privacy, Ruby was an entitled snoop—no real news there—and Andy played his cards close. You might never know how things affected him unless you watched very carefully, just as Jett was doing now.

She realized that Andy was the one who knew everything. She saw him connecting the dots, putting everything in context. Jett eyed each of them in turn and slowly raised her hand, mimicking Andy's languid greeting from yesterday.

"Hi," she said, then paused for a beat. "Yes. It's true. I can speak again. And I'm back, as you can see. I know I missed a lot of time in school, but really it's more than that, isn't it? We have a project we not only need to do, but we need to make exceptional. Since I've been gone so long, I have a lot of questions, like, who took over in my absence? Did anyone collect more data? What did you all learn? Did anyone start outlining the paper? What about the hypothesis? Where are we? What did you think when you saw our Core5 become a Core4?"

At that, Carlos burst into emphatic denial, waving his hands as if to push away the very idea. "No, Manita, *No*. Never, not once, were we a Core4. We are a Core5. *You are a part of our Core5*."

Jett stifled a laugh at how very serious he looked. He was still funny, even when he was practically yelling at her.

"So get those crazy thoughts out of your head and *tell me where. You. Were*!" Carlos pounded the table for emphasis.

Silence. They all looked at her, their faces each asking that same question.

Jett wanted to stay focused on the project, but she could see they were all distracted by the mystery surrounding her absence. She could see they weren't going to get anywhere until they had answers. With a looming deadline, Jett didn't know why they thought her story was so important. But she also saw and felt genuine concern; she no longer felt like laughing. Poor Carlos. Had he really been that worried? Had they all been?

"I'll tell you—I promise!—but we'll have to do it later," she said. "Right now we have a project to complete and we *have* to win the *top* award at Freshman Faire. So, I need to know what happened while I was gone, and I want to know how the project is going."

One glance at her teammates looking around at each other for answers and then down at their laps confirmed her suspicions: There hadn't been any progress at all. She turned to Ruby, who was doodling in her notebook.

"Ruby? You love to be in charge," Jett said. "Did you get anywhere on this? What happened while I was gone?"

Ruby just stared at her. Jett was surprised to realize that she was uncomfortable, shocked even. Evidently, Ruby liked being in the spotlight most of the time, but only on her terms. Jett smiled as Ruby shrugged her shoulders and started to fidget, looking around for backup that wasn't going to come.

Jett let out a heavy sigh and waited a bit longer. She thought about all the hours she had spent learning with the professionals at the Learning Lodge. Could she impart any of her new, hard-earned wisdom? Would they listen? She had to try.

She remembered how Ruby ignored her and left her on the ground the day she fell after retreating from the mean girls. Jett had been heartbroken when she realized that Ruby was choosing to stay with the vipers.

She fixed Ruby with a severe stare. "Looks like you didn't step up. And, as you can see, no one is covering for you this time," Jett said. "If you want to be a leader, you have to lead, Ruby. This isn't the virtual world. You aren't posing for social media. *This is real life*. You don't have a team covering for you, making you look good, doing your work for you. All right? You got that? You need to let yourself *be*, Ruby, and show us what you have to contribute."

Ruby's mouth had dropped open as she spoke. Now she sat open-jawed, staring at Jett. But Jett didn't have time to deal with Princess drama. No more waiting for someone to lead; she needed their project to be the best.

Jett turned her back on Ruby dismissively and zeroed in on her next target.

"Carlos, what did you do on this assignment? I know you had off-season practice, but this project is on-season *right now*," she said. "What did you do to move it toward the goalposts?"

Carlos shrugged nonchalantly, but his skin tone had gained a pulsing pink as a sheepish look crossed his face.

"Well, Manita, between worrying about you, practicing for the upcoming season, keeping up with the rest of my classes, working at my family's business, and trying to sort out why Ruby is so cold, I didn't get very far."

Jett didn't let up. "Really? What does not getting very far look like? Do you have more data for me? Did you maybe create a game plan for us?"

He shook his head and looked down wordlessly. But she wasn't done.

"Carlos?"

He looked up and met her eyes.

Jett laid out the truth. "You are my first 'everywhere' friend. *Ever*. And I'm sorry I worried you. I didn't tell anyone anything before I left and I didn't have my phone while I was gone, so I couldn't tell you anything until I got back. I'm sorry I scared you, but I was fine. Actually, better than fine, as you already know because my voice is back."

He smiled wanly at her as she finished up. "Here's my concern: If you let a little thing like my being gone or practice for an upcoming—not even current!—season get in your way, how do we know you're really committed to this project?"

Next Jett turned to Sam, who looked like she was enjoying this new Jett.

"Sam, did you sort out anything more for the project?"

Sam nodded cautiously. "Actually I did, but I haven't written it down yet," she said. "I thought about love and what it's like in my neighborhood, where we all look out for each other. I go to church with my Grandma and she has a whole group of people who show their love in the way they just come over and hang out. It's funny to me because I used to think only young people hung out together for no good reason. But now I know Grandma and her crew do, too. They take turns at each other's places when I'm at school or my sister is at work. I think the way they love each other is by spending time together." Sam peered at Jett. "Could that be right?"

Jett had been slapping her thigh under the table, trying to contain her excitement and enthusiasm. "I think that's it *exactly!* Actually, it goes along with something Andy and I were talking about yesterday." She nodded to him. "Are you ready to tell them what we learned?"

Andy dove into an explanation of what they had learned about love languages. All the while, Jett was unconsciously slapping her thighs. Sitting next to her, Andy noticed Jett's tic and stopped talking. He swallowed. Everyone stared. Silence engulfed them and no one spoke.

When Jett realized she was doing something atypical, she scrambled to cover her awkwardness, redirecting the focus back to the project.

"Here's the bottom line," she said. "I don't have time to do all the work myself if we're gonna win this thing. Besides, that wouldn't be fair. I'm going to do more than just compile the data, but we each need to do a part. Do you want to hear my ideas about how to divide it up?"

Everyone nodded, eager for direction.

"You're each gonna take a test right now to determine your love language, then tonight you're going to get as many people as you can to take the same test," Jett said. "Gather up their data. Those who score highest in your love language will be asked to participate further. I've written up a list of questions; if they're willing to help, you can interview them. Then bring all of this back to me. "

Jett watched as they each took out their phones, went online, and took the test. As she had suspected would be the case, each team member had a different primary love language. Good. As long as each person did their part, the data would be balanced.

Even jaded Ruby was infected with her enthusiasm. "This stupid test actually makes sense. I got time. Carlos, what did you get?"

"Who me, Linda? I'm all about the regalos, the gifts." He looked at Jett. "Your main thing is words, right? You like the words?"

"Actually, no," she said. "My primary love language is touch." She looked shyly over at Andy. "What about you?"

Andy blushed. "Mine is probably no surprise, but it's acts of service." Wanting to pass the attention to someone else, he quickly added, "Sam? You're last but not least. Tell me you're 'words' and then we've got them all covered!"

Sam gave two thumbs up, wiggling her eyebrows at him.

And there it was. Each team member had their own specialty to explore. They could do this—if everyone did their part.

"This makes sense," Ruby said. "But let's sweeten the deal. I'll give a reward to the one who collects the most data—besides me, of course, because I'll beat you all. But the one who wins second place will get highlighted in my social media—a special series about you to help you grow your own following. Yes?"

"Oh yeah, Linda! I want it. That should be me!" Carlos enthused. "Bring it on!" Sam was nodding approvingly. Andy responded with a shy smile.

With an acknowledging nod at Ruby, Jett got back to taking notes. This first day back had been full of discoveries and new directions, not all of them comfortable. Was progress usually uncomfortable? She'd have to think about that. But for now? For now, she was just glad the Core5 was a real team—and they all wanted to win.

26

LATER THAT AFTERNOON, Jett was looking at her phone as she walked across the edge of the field, her brain buried in research. She was thinking about love, particularly how touch was a primary love language. That was her focus, not only for the project, but for her life right now. It took up every moment as she tried to understand. How did people fulfill this need, this form of love? What if touch was your primary love language, but you didn't like people because they were so confusing? Would that stop you from being loving? And if you weren't a loving person, what type of person were you?

At the moment, she was researching the intersection of normal, typical, and touch. Jett stopped in her tracks as she pulled up an article that said autistic people didn't like to be touched. Definitively. She frowned. Could that be true? Always? Was that a distinct part of autism—part of its very definition—or was it only true sometimes? Either way, did that mean people on the spectrum didn't have touch as a primary love language? Or, did it need to be qualified? For instance, were girls different from boys? Did she know anyone that this data fit? It certainly seemed like a gross generalization. Maybe she'd need to create a new board to sort this out.

Jett started to walk again, musing about how she would get enough people to take the quiz. She needed to find others with touch as a primary love language, but she didn't really socialize with anyone beyond her parents and Ben. Where was she going to find people to interview? Maybe she could return to the Learning Lodge and quiz the staff.

Out of the corner of her eye, Jett saw the group of boys Carlos hung out with coming her way. They must've just finished practice. Where was Carlos? Oh, there. He was deep in conversation with the coaches. Carlos didn't notice as his friends circled around her, the obnoxious blonde one acting as ringleader. Was she supposed to greet him or something? Why? The only time he had spoken to her was when he offered to do Carlos' portion of the project. Jett wasn't sure she approved of his ethics. Was he trying to cheat or to help a friend? She crossed her arms and met his stare straight on so he would know she wasn't afraid. Should she be?

"Haven't seen you in a while, Jett," he said with a hint of challenge in his voice. "How are you?"

The other boys remained silent, inspecting her. Jett decided to be polite. No use embarrassing Blondie by asking who he was and why he was speaking to her.

"I'm good. Knee-deep in research. You?"

"Knee-deep?" he asked, letting his gaze shift down her denim-covered legs briefly. "Which project?"

"The one I'm working on with Carlos."

"You mean the one on love?" Now the boy was openly leering at her.

Jett was surprised that he remembered. She nodded curtly.

"Did Carlos come through?" he asked in a tone that she didn't understand. "Did he teach you about loooove?" He drew the word out into two or three syllables.

Maybe he could be one of her test subjects, even a candidate for an interview. That depended on his scores, of course.

"Not yet," she replied evenly. "Did you want to help?"

His brows shot up and his mouth dropped open for just a moment. Then he smirked.

"You want my help learning about love? What about Carlos?"

Jett shrugged. "What about him? He can help too. I need to learn lots. I'm researching touch right now. Are you up for it?"

The whole circle of boys began to laugh, surprising her and seemingly egging on Blondie. Did he only want to help Carlos, then?

"Sure! Maybe you want help from some of my friends, too?"

Spreading his arms wide, he turned in a circle to indicate his crew. The other boys moved in closer, gawking. "When did you..."

Suddenly Sam was there, right next to Jett, interrupting.

"Hey, Dorothy, what are you doing talking to this bozo?"

This day was just endlessly full of surprises. Jett was startled as much by Sam's assessment of Carlos' friend as she was by being called "Dorothy" in front of other people. She thought that was a private nickname, but maybe they really were "everywhere" friends! Jett smiled with delight at Sam, who kept talking in a low voice.

"Dorothy, this isn't Kansas and this isn't Oz. He's not the wizard," Sam said, and then with a glance at the circle she added, "although these may be munchkins."

Sam took her arm and began to pull. "Just in case you aren't clear, this isn't where you need to be right now," she nearly whispered into her ear. Then, more loudly: "You coming? We've got to go to that thing. You don't like being late."

Jett thought she saw Sam wink at her, but that made about as much sense as Sam fetching her for some "thing" that Jett hadn't calendared. But it was obvious that Sam needed her, so Jett decided to follow Sam's lead.

"Oh! Yeah. Right. That thing!"

She turned back to the circle of boys.

"Excuse us, please, gentlemen. We're late." As Sam pulled her away, Jett waved at the blonde boy. "Bye, Bozo," she said cheerily.

Sam giggled under her breath at something as she urged Jett along. Carlos arrived just as they left. "Hey, what did I miss?" he asked the blonde boy.

Everyone laughed at the answer she couldn't hear, but Jett didn't miss the loud smack as Carlos' fist hit the boy squarely in the jaw. She started to turn back, but Sam had launched them into a run.

"Come on, Jett! We've got to go *now*!"

27

"STOP. STOP. SAM!" Jett yelled, out of breath. She reached her arm out in a straight line, like her Mother had done in car rides at any stop sign. Jett stopped running and waited for Sam to stop as well.

"Why did we do that? Where are we going?" She peppered Sam with questions in between deep breaths. She really was winded. "Did you know Carlos hit that guy when everyone was laughing? It sounded like he hit him hard. Will the boy hit Carlos back? What if he needs us? What just happened?"

Sam was bent over, palms on her knees, also breathing hard, but now she was starting to laugh. "Wow, Jett. You really don't get it, do you?" She shook her head, grinning. "I swear—I love you, you're the best, and you'd never make it in my hood or on the streets."

None of that made any sense. Jett felt her brows draw down as she tried to figure it out, but she quickly recognized the most important part: Sam loved her. The rest of what she'd said kind of didn't matter anymore.

"Come on. Let's walk," Sam said. "I've got an 'in' to the music hall."

Pleased, Jett fell into step beside her friend. If Sam loved her, could they be best friends? What exactly did that entail? She would have to do some research. That might be a lot.

"The dudes Carlos hangs out with are just normal guys," Sam explained. Jett was glad that Sam already understood that everyone was normal. "They're like, *totally* normal. Know what I mean? They won't listen like Andy or defend like Carlos. They're not part of our Core and they wouldn't be good for data points, Jett. They would only mess up the information and confuse the final results. I promise, you want no part of any of them. Don't give them the time of day again. Okay, Jett?" Sam was emphatic.

Jett could see how serious Sam was about all of this, but it wasn't making any sense. She was doing her best to process it all; for now, though, it was clear that she was going to have to follow Sam's lead.

"Okay, but you know I didn't give them the time, right? They could find that on their phones already," she assured Sam. "But still, I promise not to give it to them, even if they ask. And I won't let them help on our project, especially since you said they would mess up our data. That is not okay! Thank you for telling me and getting me away from there. Do we really have something planned, and I just forgot, or did you need something?"

Once again, Sam looked like she was trying hard not to laugh. She laid a gentle hand on Jett's shoulder. "I do need something. I need you to listen to a new song I'm trying out. Tell me how it lands, okay? Be my audience?"

Jett jumped up and down with excitement. "Oh my goodness! Really? Like *really*, really? Can we go do that *right now*?" Without waiting to see if Sam was ready, Jett sprinted toward the music hall. She turned back to Sam. "Come on! What are you waiting for?"

When they reached the hall, Sam used her access code to open a door. They went straight to the heart of the building—to the exact spot where Jett first heard Sam's musical magic so many months ago. Gesturing for Jett to take a seat—not an easy task with excitement bubbling through her system—Sam paced around in figure eights for a bit. She looked like she was muttering something and her arms were outstretched in some sort of plea. Finally, she turned to face Jett, opened her mouth, and began to sing.

She sang and sang until pain became joy. Sam teased out notes that flirted with the skin of Jett's arm; Jett put a hand to her forearm and looked down, trying to contain herself. Sam smiled and moved to a new song, one filled with hope and courage. Unconsciously, Jett rose from the floor and raised her arms toward the sun filtering in through the overhead windows. As Sam's magic enveloped her, Jett slowly turned in circles, bathing in the warmth of this moment. She felt free.

When the private concert ended, Sam breathed in deeply and then exhaled slowly. She reached for the water bottle in her backpack. Jett twirled to a stop. The silence was full and Jett felt her heart expand.

"Wow, Sam. Just—wow."

They stared at each other for a moment before Sam ducked her head. She looked like she was shy or embarrassed or something. Jett couldn't understand why that would be so. Had they not just experienced the same magic? What could possibly be embarrassing in that?

"Sam, where in the world did you learn to sing like that, and why do you look so shy right now? Do you have any idea how magical that was?" Jett had so many more questions, but she sensed she should keep them to herself for now.

With her head still bowed, Sam shrugged. Jett worried that Sam was retreating, like she was closing in on herself. To her relief, Sam responded.

"If I tell you, you can't tell anyone, okay?" she said. "What we share in this music hall has to stay right here, got it? Promise me."

Jett certainly understood privacy. She nodded solemnly.

"My world isn't like yours, Jett. It just isn't." Sam used a finger for each point she was trying to make. She started with one. "You live with two parents. I live with none." She held up finger number two. "You probably live somewhere super-fancy, super-posh, like Ruby and Carlos and, I'm guessing, Andy. But me? I don't live next door to Richie Rich. I live in a one-bedroom walkup with my Grams and my sister." Sam paused to let it sink in. "Do you even know what a walkup is?"

Jett shook her head no. She concentrated hard on everything Sam was saying. She wanted desperately to understand.

Sam's third finger went up. "I take a train and two buses to get here. What do you take?"

Jett opened her mouth to answer, but Sam held her hand up for silence before Jett could make a sound.

A fourth finger joined the others. "You want to know about my singing, about where and how. Well let's start with why." Sam took a deep, audible breath and studied Jett somberly. "Remember, you promised you won't tell. Real friends don't tell."

Jett nodded silently, focusing intensely. Sam laced her fingers, flexed them back, then held her arms straight out in front of her body. Her shoulders went back and her jaw ticked. This must be really private, Jett thought, something no one else here knew. She couldn't fathom what it would be.

"I learned to sing to cover up the sounds I heard outside our home," Sam said, closing her eyes and tilting her face up into a beam of sunlight. "Sometimes I sing over sirens and gunshots. Sometimes I sing to drown out drug dealers and addicts. Sometimes I sing just to be sure I'm still alive."

She opened her eyes and turned toward Jett. "Some days I sing with my sister. She taught me everything I know." Her gaze shifted to look out across the empty hall. Jett wondered why Sam looked so sad.

"Miya—that's my sister—taught me how to sing in public so we can bring home money for our Grandma," she said. "We sound so good together."

Sam smiled even as she bowed her head and looked at her hands. She blinked rapidly.

Jett watched in horror and fascination. Was Sam crying? Why? She didn't know what to do, so she just listened.

"And that's good, but now I need to get ready to do this on my own," she said, squaring her shoulders and unknotting her fingers. "Miya auditioned and scored a role in the touring cast of *Hamilton*. She'll be gone before you and I get back to school after summer break."

Sam took another deep breath and held it briefly before blowing it out slowly through her nostrils. Jett waited. She knew that sound. It was the sound of a tender truth reaching for exposure. "I need more songs so I can earn us more money," Sam said softly. I mean, we do all right, but what if, when Miya's gone, what if it's not enough?"

With that, Sam looked directly at Jett. Jett remained still, head cocked to the side as she tried to make sense of all the new information. A flush of color began to rise in Sam's face.

"Miya says she'll send money home, but what if she can't? I've been practicing all year on BART to and from school. I hold out my hat and I tell people, 'I'm going to sing for you. If you enjoy it or the music touches you in some way, all I ask is that you please contribute what you can.'" Sam shrugged. "It buys me lunch and pays for me to get here every day. Plus, I get to sing. I sing to drown out what I don't want to remember. I sing to bring a smile to faces that don't have them. I sing to relate to strangers. I sing for those who want to, but can't. I am their voice."

Sam stopped and looked at Jett, waiting to see how she would react.

Jett could feel it even as she was rummaging in her bag. She pulled out four twenties and held them out to Sam. The money wasn't a big deal to Jett, but as she saw Sam back up she realized it might be a very big deal to Sam.

Sam looked horrified. "What are you doing? I didn't tell you my story so you would give me money. I don't want it."

Confused, Jett continued to hold out the cash, but lowered it a little. "But you just sang for me, a whole private concert and everything! I want to contribute, just like you said. Besides, if you take it, maybe you'll take a request."

They stared at each other. Jett gulped, but held her gaze. She hoped Sam could see how important this was to her and how much she wanted Sam to sing her request.

Finally, Sam quirked a smile at her. "Okay, Dorothy, but you're supposed to sing 'Over the Rainbow.' Do you need me to teach it to you?"

Jett's jaw dropped. "Like, for real? You would teach me how to sing? You could teach me your magic? I could sing 'Over the Rainbow' someday?"

Sam nodded—and plucked the cash from her hand.

Jett thought she might explode with joy. She jumped up and down, clapping.

"That is awesome! But I didn't pay you for that—yet," Jett enthused. "For now, I want you to sing that Andra Day song 'Rise Up' for me. Do you know it?"

Sam was grinning at her. "Know it? Yeah, Jett. I know it, my sister and I sing it together all the time—or whenever we need hope. It's our home song. Do you want to hear my version?"

Jett sat down again, nodding eagerly. She made a mental note to order red "Dorothy" shoes, noting as she did that Sam was pacing, in circles this time. Pacing seemed to help center Sam before she sang. At last, she slowed and Jett closed her eyes as Sam opened her mouth. The magic traveled from Sam and wrapped around Jett. It filled her heart. Sam loved her. Jett was going to learn how to be a best friend and then maybe Sam would let her be that, too. She would rise—a thousand times a day.

AT HOME IN the family office, Jett stared at a blank wall. It was project time and she couldn't wait to get answers. Her Core5 had supplied tons of data for her to compile. And just in time, too. The presentation was less than a week away. She had what she needed to clarify their thoughts and sort some answers. Jett was a very happy girl indeed.

Mother would give her a tough time, but because this work was team-related? Jett hoped she might give her a little less grief about not being a popular kid yet.

Jett started looking through the stacks of information, their preliminary tallies. Everyone had done their part securing solid data. Jett found it interesting that no obvious pattern had emerged, but that was exciting, too. What would they uncover?

Jett thought back on how hard it had been to find people for her part of the study. She didn't like approaching strangers and she didn't socialize with many people. When she couldn't come up with a solution, she'd finally broken down and explained her dilemma to Daddio. And her Dad—her crazy, awesome Dad—had stepped up.

"I have an idea, if you want me to help," he'd said. "You know all you have to do is ask."

All she could do was nod, and so he had taken the quiz to work. Everyone in the office who filled it out got a reward. Daddio used this excuse to pass out animal ball poppers to willing participants. Those who qualified for further research were given the option to be interviewed by Jett. His administrative assistant set up all the interviews and Jett spent many hours in "her office"—also known as a client meeting room—collecting more information. Her Dad swore all the participants did it to help, but she suspected there were tangible 'thank you' gifts for helping his daughter. Jett smiled to herself; after all, his primary love language was gifts.

Back home, she divided the data into the five categories and started putting it all up on the wall. Next, she read through all the interviews and put up the most compelling examples, each under their matching category. When the sun went down and it was time to turn on the lights, Jett jumped at the sound of the garage door opening. Then she heard them.

"Honey? You home? Your wayward parents have arrived! Where are you hiding?" Daddio was always joking around.

"I'm in the Den of Data," she yelled back with a thrill of pride at her clever response.

"Don't you mean the Love Lounge?" He popped his head in. "Pizza tonight? It is Friday, after all."

"Yes, please!"

She jumped up and looked at her Dad, who was taking a long look at her wall of information.

"Is this what you were trying to figure out before Yoda left?" he asked. "The info you had on the boards in here?"

It felt like dangerous territory, so she simply nodded and gripped her hands together. She didn't want to talk about it. She just stared at her wall, praying silently he would leave it alone and she would find the answers she sought.

No such luck.

"Hey, Doodlebug, I just want you to know I'm sorry," he started, coming all the way into the room. "I didn't understand how it looked to you. I wish I could have figured that out and maybe we wouldn't have lost so much time, you know?"

He was staring at her back; Jett could feel it. She continued to stare at the wall. He cleared his throat.

"In any event, I am sorry I let you down. Please forgive me?"

Forgive him? For what? For not having the same brain type and not having any idea what she was thinking? She turned to face him, took two steps toward him—and that was all he needed to open his arms and bend forward to engulf her in one of his super Dad hugs, her favorite place to be. She could see his eyes swimming in tears.

"All right, Bug," he said gruffly, releasing her and quickly swiping a hand under his nose. "I see you have a lot of work to do. Let me know if you need any help. I'll be the one eating all the pizza." And with that, he turned and left.

Jett walked slowly back to her wall and stared without seeing. If people spoke each other's language, not just learned their own, but learned the top love language for each of the important people in their lives, would it make life better?

That would have to be a follow-up experiment, another hypothesis to test. This year they would just have to explain the not-so-basic basics of how to be a loving person.

After a while, she asked her parents to listen as she practiced the presentation. Daddio gave it two thumbs up, but Mother had her usual cautionary criticism. "Are you sure you're the best one to represent your team? I mean, surely, don't you have someone more social? What about that Ruby Steffano or that heartthrob soccer kid, Carlos?"

Jett felt herself wither. It was obvious Mother still thought she needed help. So she reworked the presentation and gave parts to each member of the team. They would still need a narrator, but at least it took the pressure off of one presenter. Jett knew Ruby wouldn't object. And she had put together all the data. Jett sighed in defeat. Yeah, maybe her Mom was right.

———➤ ✦ ≺———

JETT HAD SPENT the entire weekend compiling data and putting together a solid presentation. In just a few minutes, she was going to show her team. First, though, she needed to see Dr. W. She had a challenge for him. Jett knew this was unusual, but so was her team. She headed to the counselor's office full of hope, curiosity, and determination. Dr W didn't know what their meeting was about. He didn't know what was about to hit him. Jett did; she bounced with excitement.

WHEN SHE ARRIVED late to class, she found Ruby pacing and the rest of her Core5 fidgeting anxiously.

"Jett, you got it, right? You solved the riddle and made sense of all the crazy info we gave you?" Ruby asked, clearly thinking such a feat was impossible. Jett just smiled at her. How little Ruby knew. She focused instead on the rest of the team.

"Hey guys. Sorry I was late. Maybe it wasn't my best decision, but I had to stop by Dr. W's office first." Jett wondered if any of them saw the extra sparkle in her eyes. "Anyone else here doubt my ability to pull this off? Do we need to work through that? Or can we just skip to the good stuff?"

Carlos jumped up and clapped. "Manita! I knew you could do it! What's next? What do you need me to do?"

She lowered her voice. "Let's take it outside," she said. They trooped out together with a nod of permission from Ms. Diaz. Quickly, Jett outlined her plan. Moods rose as they began to understand what Jett had put together, weaving all the different sections into one cohesive presentation.

Lining the walls of the hallway were photos of winning teams from the past. None of them looked particularly happy or cohesive. Had they really considered themselves Core5? Were they still? Jett made a note to herself to find out, once this was all over. She didn't want to end up like them, looking serious, sad and disjointed. They weren't Core5, not like her team was. She knew she wanted to win and she wanted her team to win. They had to. They were the real deal. People needed to see a new normal, a real team. They needed what she had, what they had together.

After a pause, she turned to Ruby. With more than 14 million followers now, Jett knew that Ruby was the most qualified to get their project noticed. And people needed to notice.

"Ruby, you're the obvious candidate to tie this all together and represent our team," she said. "I want you to do the initial hypothesis and wrap-up. Okay? Everyone agree?"

No one spoke, not even Ruby. Sam and Andy shared a look. They shook their heads simultaneously. Then Carlos joined them. Jett held her breath. What now?

"No way," Ruby replied. "I can't be the face of this. I have other things on my plate and I think I need to just do my section on words."

This was not what Jett expected. How could she get Ruby—who always thought she knew everything—to change her mind? Jett's mind spun as Ruby enlisted her teammates in the mutiny. "Right, guys? We have enough to do just doing our parts. Who's doing what?"

"I'm covering service," offered Andy.

"I've got words," Sam added.

"And I get to be all about the *regalos*, the gifts! I love me some gifts," Carlos enthused.

"And I'll be awesome talking about quality time. That leaves you with touch and the general presentation," Ruby said. "Can you do that for us, Jett? Be the face? I mean, honestly, you seriously worked some magic already. Maybe we *can* win this thing."

Jett's vision blurred with tears. She slowly nodded. The lump in her throat made it impossible to speak right now, but she would. She would speak for them all, including herself. Jett only hoped she could do this justice, for all of them. *They* were the Core5.

29

THE FRESHMAN FAIRE was held in a big auditorium at the historic Palace of Fine Arts. Each team had its own table and visitors wandered from project to project to learn about a topic of interest. Jett's team members were busy defending their thesis and rousing curiosity by still collecting data, encouraging visitors to take the quiz. As their results were tallied, each visitor was offered an interview with the teammate in charge of their primary love language. Sometimes it was a bit frenetic, but no one declined the invitation; each person learned more about themselves and how they process love.

When it was time for the presentations, Jett's Core5 continued their unique approach. Instead of one student heading to the podium, the entire team moved in unison. They stood together as Jett began. She saw her parents standing in the front of the crowd, her Dad's smile giving her courage. She avoided direct eye contact as she began.

"For our project, we decided to sort out the definition of love. I'm not sure an entire school year was enough time for us, but we're starting to get there."

Appreciative laughter rippled through the crowd.

"Each of my teammates has a specific love language that they are particularly well versed in. We have divided not only the work, but also this presentation, into sections where you will hear from each expert. Our hypothesis is that love, while considered universal, is expressed in many different ways. These ways can be broken down into five categories. For now, I'm going to pass the time over to Carlos so he can tell you about the language of gifts, or *regalos,* as he likes to call them. As he discusses this, ask yourself: Does this sound like you or like someone you know?" Jett turned towards her beaming, very first "everywhere" friend. "Are you ready?"

"Manita! Thank you! You know I am!" He kissed her cheek as she walked by. Out of the corner of her eye, Jett saw her Mother's look of shock. She wondered what Mother was thinking. But Carlos was already well into his part of the presentation, so Jett shifted her focus back where it belonged.

Each member of the Core5 brought passion and story to their section. Some made the audience laugh and others made them cry. Jett was excited to see how each one affected the listeners. She was surprised to see how rapt the audience was as they presented their hard-won knowledge.

Other competitors left their own booths and came to listen. Things were going far better than she had expected!

Jett spotted Ben watching from the back of the room, and he winked. Her heart soared. Ben, her neighbor, her old companion, her first mentor about love—she was so glad that he had gotten her card. A few days ago, she had left him a handwritten note inviting him to the presentation. Jett had left it on his doorstep, where he couldn't miss it, but she hadn't been sure how he would react. Why was he standing all the way in the back? Should she go off script and mention him in her final story?

She raised her hand in a small wave and Ben waved back. He folded his arms then, but not before giving her a thumbs up and a small, sad smile. She wondered about that. Did he miss her as much as she missed him? Would he get the message if she told everyone? She debated how she could brighten his smile without disobeying Mother's explicit ban on direct contact with an older, single man, for whatever reason. Jett was staring off into the crowd, seeing nothing but the puzzle in her mind, when Sam nudged her gently. It was her turn again. Andy was wrapping up.

"And now we're ready for the final love language—touch," Andy said with a flourish. "Jett, are you ready to bring it home?"

Smiling, she put herself front and center and placed her hands on either side of the podium. She was nervous at the thought of doing what felt right, and going off-script. *Here goes nothing*, she thought.

"Earlier this year, I met my neighbor Ben and his pup Yoda. We had great conversations and he helped me start to put a frame around this whole thing called love. It was difficult for me to grasp, but he never laughed at me or made me feel stupid. As we spent more time together, I found myself wanting to hug him sometimes, but I never did. Ben gave me room to consider how love applies in real life. I watched him with his pup. I watched him share his thoughts with a stranger. I watched him give and receive love, and I learned. Yoda is gone now and although we no longer see each other on a regular basis, I want Ben to know he is loved, not just Yoda. Ben is loved by many, but also by me, too. Thank you, Ben."

Jett turned her attention to the front of the audience.

"The natural, healthy physical expression of love is something I share only with people I love, and not socially without forethought. It's truly how I speak my love. And if I had our time to do over again, I would have hugged Ben, at least once. I know there are others like me because I interviewed a number of them.

"What I find surprising is how different people express their love in ways I wouldn't have guessed. I am grateful we have started sorting out our own love languages and I encourage you to do the same. Stop by our booth if you need some help getting started. But, more importantly, take the time to learn how you give love and how those you love want to receive it. I think that's our next step. I think we need to compare notes and learn how to speak each other's love languages.

"For example, if I know that time is important to Ruby, I can use that knowledge to build her up and show her I know she matters. She could have taken over this presentation and presented something to rock the social-media world. She even was offered the opportunity to do so, but she turned it down to ensure our group project was a team presentation, not just a spotlight on her." Jett turned and smiled at Ruby, who ducked her head and smiled, looking away.

Jett turned to the rest of the group. "I want each of you to know that you have taught me about love, and I am grateful. I want to wrap up our presentation by inviting our audience to *learn* more, and then for all of us to *do* more. I want for all of us to express more love into this world, because we all deserve it."

Jett stepped back and Sam's hand found hers. Sam already was holding onto Andy, who was holding on to Ruby, who was holding onto Carlos.

The room erupted in a thunder of applause. Jett looked out and saw her Dad on his feet clapping the loudest. He looked so proud. Mother looked mildly shocked, but also pleased, if a bit confused. Did she not understand something? Jett would have to ask her later. Jett walked off the platform with the rest of the group, fielding congratulations from a sea of unfamiliar faces. She looked for Ben, but he was gone. She didn't know his love language but she hoped he had gotten her message.

As she made her way back to the team table, she was inundated with questions popping like popcorn. Jett raised her hand. "Order!" she called out. "Order, please, I want to answer questions but I need to hear them one at a time." With a quick glance around, she realized her teammates were fielding just as many questions. As she struggled to answer, she started repeatedly pinching the base of her neck. She didn't even realize she was doing it; she just knew she felt better as a result.

Wow. They had done it. Her team had given their presentation and the response was overwhelming.

Carlos, who was standing nearby, silently reached out to her and gently took her hand.

"This is my Manita. She is a genius, and I need for you all to give us some more space, okay?" To her surprise, it worked. People stopped crowding so closely, but he didn't let go of her hand. Jett looked down at their hands and then back up at the crowd. One by one, her classmates stopped talking and came to gather around them. Ruby spoke up as she stepped in next to Carlos.

"Thank you all for coming, and thank you for spending time at our table. We have much to tell you and I'm not sure how far we'll get, but we're a team now, and we're going to finish this as a team. I'll take the question in the back from the Dad in the yellow sweatshirt."

And just like that, the Core5 displayed a new level of love, acceptance, and understanding. Ruby glanced at Jett and pursed her lips, lifting her eyebrows. Jett chuckled as Ruby turned back to the Q&A session.

At the end of the day, Dr. W escorted the panel of judges to their table. "We're supposed to announce from the stage who the winner of this year's Freshman Faire is, but I think it's pretty clear already," he said, smiling broadly. "You still have most of the people in the room swarming your table and awaiting your wisdom. I just want to confirm you won."

He turned to Jett with a broad wink.

"And Jett? I haven't forgotten. You negotiated a special prize for your team in the event you won. You are one extraordinary team and I will coordinate that prize with you all later. Congratulations!" With another wink to Jett, he blended back into the crowd as the Core5 clamored around Jett.

"What did you do?" Carlos asked.

"I don't know," Sam said, "but I bet it's epic."

Jett smiled mysteriously.

"Well, I just... I asked Dr. W if he could take us all on a field trip to Safari West if we won and he said yes! I kind of tricked him because I reminded him how many teams were competing and that we were just one team and what were the odds, but he said yes. Soooo—private zoo tour anyone?"

It was the group's turn to jump up and down with excitement. Jett thought she heard someone squeal.

"OhmiGAWD, Jett, really? Safari West? Will we go on a jeep safari thingy and everything? Think we can go this summer?" asked Ruby, who suddenly looked like just another girl, not a superstar. She was ecstatic. Jett had contributed to that. She was so proud.

Andy weighed in next. "Think we can go this week, or very soon anyway? I'm supposed to go with my family on our annual adventure but I don't want to miss this. Way cool, Jett! How did you know to ask him for that?"

She raised her eyebrows at him. "It all started with a few pictures in his office and the day you wore giraffe socks, Andy," she said. As she told the story, she saw her parents silently observing and waiting for her. "One sec, guys. My parentals are waiting for me." Detaching herself from the group, she Jett walked over to them. "So? What did you think?"

"Kiddo, I'm in awe," Daddio began. "Where did you get those mad skills? I didn't know you could do that! Wanna come work at the firm? We could use a good negotiator."

"I don't understand what just happened," Mother chimed in. "Are those your friends? They seem like real friends, not just teammates. Are they?"

Jett waved at her Core5 and then shrugged at her parents. "Thanks, Dad and I don't know, Mom. I haven't tested the theory. I mean, I *think* three of them are 'everywhere' friends, but I'm still trying to sort out the last one. Any tips on how I can tell?"

Mother looked nonplussed. "'Everywhere' friends, Jett? What are those? What does that even mean? Can you tell me more? Maybe we should schedule a session with Amy so she can help you figure it out."

Jett held up a hand to stop that line of thinking. "Mom, thank you, but no thank you. I have my medical team and we are sorting out everything I need to lead the best Jett life. I'm sure Amy has a lot to say, but maybe you should talk to her. I'm good with Dr. W for now."

The growing tension was cut short as the loudspeaker crackled over everything. "This year, the Freshman Faire's top award goes to a team from Ms. Diaz's class—the Core5 who focused on "How to Be a Loving Person" wins the day! Team, please come up to the front of the room and claim your prize."

"*Regalos!*" enthused Carlos "I think we get something!" He started to sprint across the room, still talking, when he realized his team wasn't with him. He ran back. "Hey! What's taking you so long? That's our cue. They're calling for us. Come on!" He grabbed both Ruby's and Jett's hands this time. Jett reached out for Sam, who reached out for Andy, and they all walked up together, to claim their prize.

This year, the photo of the winning team was a little different. It was the first time in the history of the Presidio Prep Freshman Faire that all members of a winning team were holding hands and smiling.

30

ON THE MORNING of the last day of her freshman year, Jett was not smiling. It had been rough so far. All the way to school, Mother kept nattering on about how typical is normal. And not typical? Well, it just wasn't. And, according to Mother, Jett needed to try harder. If she would just "try," Mother was sure Jett could magically become typical.

Jett was tired of the argument. She was tired of the insistence. Most of all, she was tired of the belief that Jett was wrong. Wrong in her very being.

What about genius? What about the claims her brain worked exceptionally well? What about her wins? If typical was normal and that level of performance was above typical, then was she supposed to be ashamed of that, too? How come that was handed to her like praise, like something she should be proud of, but not the other ways she wasn't typical? Seriously. All of this made her tired, cranky even, and definitely wanting to crawl back into her cave of quilts.

Standing outside of the building housing her Foundations class, she stared out toward the bay. Sailboats dotted the water. She memorized the geometry of the Golden Gate Bridge. Symmetry calmed chaos. Jett wondered, not for the first time, why the Golden Gate Bridge was painted a rusty orange-red, not actually gold. Andy stood patiently next to her. She looked at his neon rainbow socks and smiled.

"Jett?" said Andy. "Are you ready? I've heard today we're supposed to be at school but not really *do* school, if that makes sense. So, tell me what you have planned for this summer?"

Jett wondered whether it would be TMI to tell Andy she was crafting the next levels of argument against Mother's assertions. Did he understand what it was like to consistently be told, "you are awesome, now please go change"? Jett shrugged and pulled on the strap of her backpack. "Same old, same old. You?"

Andy was more animated than she had remembered him being in a while. Jett didn't know if it was because she knew him better, so he was more comfortable around her, or because he was really so excited about several months apart. She inspected his socks. Sure enough, they held clues. Today Andy wore socks with wildly colorful stripes and thought bubbles on them exclaiming "Wow," "Yes," and "Totally." She tuned back into his words.

"And after that, my sister is totally going to take over the planning, which means we'll probably end up swimming a lot. Anamika is part dolphin!" He laughed quietly to himself as they walked on in companionable silence.

Jett was puzzled for a moment, but then matched his smile. He was joking. His sister wasn't part dolphin. That statement had made no sense to her. Maybe he was checking to see if she was listening?

"I need to meet Anamika. I've always wanted to meet someone who is part dolphin."

She maintained eye contact with him, which was a struggle, but she was hoping he didn't see her brain spinning. Jett tried to sort out if her response was a good one. Would he see she was trying to joke back? Would he know the parts that were true, like wanting to meet Anamika?

Jett looked away as she felt someone else join them. Not a moment too soon. The enthusiasm met her flat mood.

"Hey, hey, hey!" greeted Carlos. "Are you guys so excited about summer? What's everyone doing? Me? I'm mostly working with my Pops at the new food trucks he put together for my Mamá and her crew. And playing soccer, of course. Andy, I heard you say you are going to be swimming a lot. Where? Maybe we can meet up and hang out, swimming together?"

Jett sighed. She wanted to swim. First, she wanted a nap, but she also wanted to spend the summer swimming with her friends. Would it be rude for her to insist they invite her instead of talking about it in front of her?

Ruby had fallen into step with them as the group walked across campus. Jett hadn't even noticed her until she spoke up.

"I'm sure you two would love to see me in a swimsuit, but I'm not coming unless you make room for my crew."

Ruby looked at Jett and Sam, who had just joined them. "Swimming? Did someone say swimming? I bet with enough notice I can make it, too, but *not* if you invite Ruby's entourage. No way! It's Core5 or crap. Okay?"

That did it. Now Jett's head was swimming. This was moving too fast. Was she supposed to volunteer input? Was this open to all of them, then? She thought Carlos was speaking to Andy. He had commented on Andy's plans, after all. Would anyone even notice if she kept silent and didn't talk about the summer? How could they all be so excited about so much unstructured, unplanned, unproductive time?

"Hey! We should go over to the greens!" Carlos said "The Off the Grid food trucks are there. We could get something yum and I'm starving. You?" He looked expectantly at the group. Some were nodding, some were shrugging, but Jett was silent. She was still processing the last social dilemma.

Carlos didn't notice. "Come on! I think they even have the cotton candy truck and the churros. You ever have those before? I might pass out if we don't go."

Sam glanced at Jett, who was the only one who would know that Sam may not have enough money on her to afford a trip to the food trucks. Jett stopped walking as she tried to make sense of the constantly shifting conversation. Sam backtracked to check on her.

"You okay, Dorothy? I see you're wearing some cool new shoes."

Jett's sparkly red Keds made her smile every time she looked at them. She was *so* gonna learn how to be a best friend to Sam. That would be her summer project, she decided. Sam deserved it and maybe, just maybe, she did too. It didn't matter how much work it would take to learn how. Jett wanted to put in the effort to let Sam know she loved her, too. That's what friends did.

As she stood apart with Sam, who was patiently waiting for her to speak, Jett saw the other three stop. Ruby said something that made the boys laugh. And they waited. As Jett tried to catch up in her brain, she wondered if she should go along with them. She wondered if Sam needed singing money.

Under her breath so no one else could hear, Jett checked in on Sam. "Did you make enough for this? Can I give you some singing money and you'll owe me a song?"

Sam put her arm around her shoulders. "Aw, Dorothy. I'm good, actually. I've got it. I just want you to be good, too. You good?"

Jett felt the warmth of inclusion and nodded. She was torn. Did she go home now? Sam had what she needed, after all.

Carlos, Ruby, and Andy walked back to them. Carlos—over the top, fun-loving Carlos—spoke up first. "Hey, Manita! What's the problem? Aren't you hungry? I can eat for you if you don't like it. Why are you making me wait? Are you not feeling well? I need to introduce you to dulce de leche churros! Oh, or maybe the ones with sweet crema...please? Come on! I'm waiting for you." He grabbed her hand.

Jett looked up at the expectant faces and decided. Mother and those doubts she planted and watered? They would have to wait. Her friends were right here, and they needed food. Jett smiled and started walking with them. They loved her and she loved them right back.

But even more important? Jett knew it.

AUTHOR'S NOTE

YAY! You're here!
You've completed Freshman Year at Presidio Prep.
Feel good? Ready for Sophomore Year?
Then join the Core5 in SEEKING SAFETY.

To ensure your enrollment,
go to JettHarper.com & sign up.
Can't wait to see you there!

xx
Emme Grange for the Core5

P.S. Why not bring others along?
Leaving a review or posting on social media
helps people know we're a fit.
Your thoughts matter!

ACKNOWLEDGEMENTS

I hardly know where to begin. So many people have made this debut possible, from the technical team to the emotional support. If I listed you all, this section would be longer than the book. Please know you are cherished, named here or not.

That being true, I must give a special thanks to my Mom, my first Superfan, who is NOT a Kathy. :-) I am grateful to Savannah Gilbo for keeping me on track, and Kylie Sek of Cover Culture for honing the message through conscious cover design. Stephanie Anderson of Alt 19 Creative used her mastery for interior layout & design, and Janet Rae-Dupree poured over every line. My Soul Squad cheers me on and keeps me sane. Sometimes.

Having them in my corner? I know what it's like to be loved, valued and safe. Thank you.

ABOUT THE AUTHOR

Emme Grange lives on stories of hope, on tales that tell us *we can*. She believes we don't have to change to be good enough. We already are, just by being ourselves.

She spent years searching for the missing manual, "How to Be Normal." Emme knows what it's like to be a reluctant rebel, a modern misfit, a peculiar person. She writes for anybody who needs a story of acceptance and everyone needing a story of encouragement.

CPSIA information can be obtained
at www.ICGtesting.com
Printed in the USA
BVHW051329120821
614283BV00012B/1142